HOTHOUSE EARTH

THE CLIMATE CRISIS AND THE IMPORTANCE OF CARBON NEUTRALITY

STEPHANIE SAMMARTINO MCPHERSON

TWENTY-FIRST CENTURY BOOKS / MINNEAPOLIS

FOR YOUNG PEOPLE EVERYWHERE WHO RECOGNIZE THE URGENCY OF THE ENVIRONMENTAL CRISIS, CHERISH THE BEAUTY OF THE EARTH, AND DEMAND CLIMATE ACTION NOW

Special thanks to Dr. Carlos E. Del Castillo, Oceanographer, for reviewing the text. Thanks also to Shaina Olmanson for expert editorial guidance, to Domenica Di Piazza for starting me on this project, and to my husband Richard for his unfailing support and encouragement.

Twenty-First Century Books™
An imprint of Lerner Publishing Group, Inc.
241 First Avenue North
Minneapolis, MN 55401 USA

For reading levels and more information, look up this title at www.lernerbooks.com.

Designer: Lindsey Owens
Main body text set in Adobe Garamond Pro.
Typeface provided by Adobe Systems.

Library of Congress Cataloging-in-Publication Data

Names: McPherson, Stephanie Sammartino, author.
Title: Hothouse earth : the climate crisis and the importance of carbon neutrality / Stephanie
    Sammartino McPherson.
Description: Minneapolis : Twenty-First Century Books, [2021] | Includes bibliographical
    references and index. | Audience: Ages 13–19 | Audience: Grades 10–12 | Summary: "The
    past, present, and future of Earth is a result of climate change. Climate change affects our
    everyday lives, and scientists and young people are looking into what we can do to fix it."—
    Provided by publisher.
Identifiers: LCCN 2019046586 (print) | LCCN 2019046587 (ebook) | ISBN 9781541579170 (library
    binding) | ISBN 9781728401577 (ebook)
Subjects: LCSH: Climatic changes—Juvenile literature.
Classification: LCC QC981.8.C5 M396 2021 (print) | LCC QC981.8.C5 (ebook) | DDC
    363.738/74—dc23

LC record available at https://lccn.loc.gov/2019046586
LC ebook record available at https://lccn.loc.gov/2019046587

Manufactured in the United States of America
1-47186-47903-8/26/2020

TABLE OF CONTENTS

CHAPTER ONE

THE FACE OF CLIMATE CHANGE

Constance Okollet had never experienced anything like the torrential rains that devastated Uganda in 2007. Houses toppled. Crops washed away or rotted in the standing water. "Floods like we've never seen before came and swept up everything," she would recall two years later. As the waters receded, mosquitoes bred in huge numbers and spread malaria among the hungry, homeless villagers. Five members of Okollet's family became ill. Contaminated drinking water sickened more villagers with cholera. Many people died.

Survivors depended on the government to provide the seeds they needed to resume their farming. But after the rains, drought set in. The newly planted crops shriveled and dried up. More people died of starvation. Ugandans couldn't help but ask themselves why this was happening to them. Many feared they were being punished.

Okollet did what she could, forming a network of women to help one another through the crisis. She took their concerns and stories of suffering to the local council, which provided seeds, fertilizer, and better farming equipment. She started a credit union so women could take out small loans for medicine, flour, or other needs.

But the year 2009 brought more misery—another lengthy drought followed by pounding rains. The Okollets' cows died. Their kitchen and their latrine were lost in the raging floods. Determined to fight for the well-being of her family and the other people in her country and to learn everything she could, Okollet attended a meeting held by Oxfam in a nearby village. Oxfam is a nongovernmental organization dedicated to ending world poverty.

Flooding in Uganda's Teso subregion left fields waterlogged and ruined crops.

Okollet was an eloquent spokesperson for her people, sharing their hardships and misery. She spoke so forcefully that one week later, a representative from the organization asked her to attend another meeting. This time, she would have to travel 130 miles (209 km) to Kampala, the capital of Uganda.

There, the same words came up over and over again. Okollet had never heard them before. "But what is this climate change?" she asked at last.

THE GREENHOUSE EFFECT

What Okollet learned saddened and alarmed her. Oxfam officials explained that pollution created by wealthy nations was changing the climate of the whole planet. It was the continuation of what started many years earlier when factories began releasing carbon dioxide (CO_2) into the environment. Here is why it has such a destructive impact:

These boys waded through the overflowing Achwra River in Uganda after the record rainfalls and devastating floods in September 2007. With swollen waterways like this one covering roads, it is difficult for emergency aid to reach the many people who need assistance.

The sun's energy travels to Earth, warming the land and seas. Some of this energy returns to the atmosphere as infrared radiation, or heat. Nitrogen and oxygen, the gases that make up the bulk of Earth's atmosphere do not absorb this heat. Instead, they allow it to pass back into space. However, there are other gases in the air, including CO_2. Carbon dioxide does absorb the infrared radiation, preventing it from

CLIMATE HERO CONSTANCE OKOLLET

When she first learned about climate change at an Oxfam meeting, Constance Okollet knew she had to do something. "Why do they (people in wealthy nations) do this to us?" she asked. "Can we talk to these people? Can't they reduce the pollution?" Aware of her strong desire to help her people, an Oxfam representative asked her to speak at a meeting in London. Okollet had never flown before or seen many modern conveniences such as automatic doors and lights. She had never spoken before a large audience, and she was frankly scared. But she stood up and shared her story with honesty and deep feeling. More speeches followed, including one to an international audience of lawmakers.

Okollet's London trip was only the beginning. Since then she has participated in panel discussions and met with women from all over the world. She has taken part in UN Climate Change Conferences from Copenhagen to Paris to Marrakech. As a member of Climate Wise Women, an organization that encourages women suffering the effects of climate change firsthand to speak out, she has toured the United States and Europe.

"I ask the leaders of the rich countries to take action to reduce their carbon emissions so that we can look forward to rains to plant our crops without having to face floods that wash them away," Okollet wrote in the Guardian newspaper in 2009. "And I ask them to help my community fight the climate change that destroys our houses, increases diseases and stops our children from attending schools. That's all I am asking on behalf of my fellow villagers."

Constance Okollet (*right*) and Shorbanu Khatun (*left*) examine an ice sculpture of a Kenyan Maasai warrior while attending the UN Climate Change Conference (UNCCC) in Copenhagen, Denmark, in 2009. Okollet and Khatun are both climate witnesses, or people whose lives are impacted by the changing climate.

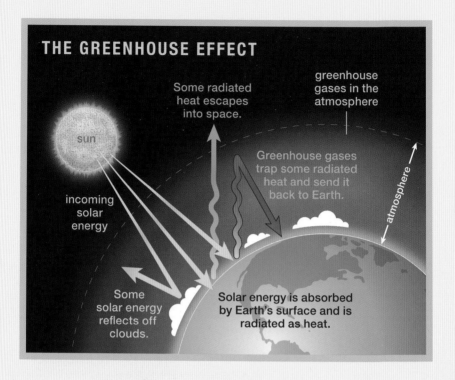

THE GREENHOUSE EFFECT

greenhouse gases in the atmosphere

Some radiated heat escapes into space.

sun

Greenhouse gases trap some radiated heat and send it back to Earth.

incoming solar energy

atmosphere

Some solar energy reflects off clouds.

Solar energy is absorbed by Earth's surface and is radiated as heat.

escaping back into space. The more carbon dioxide in the atmosphere, the more heat is trapped.

In discussing the role of CO_2 and other gases that contribute to climate change, scientists frequently speak of the "greenhouse," or warming, effect. Since the glass walls of a greenhouse hold heat inside the room, carbon dioxide and the other heat-holding gases such as water vapor, methane, nitrous oxide, and ozone are often called greenhouse gases. Rising and falling naturally over millennia, these gases play a critical role in regulating Earth's temperatures. Without their moderating effect, Earth's average temperature would be about 0°F (–18°C). Many plants and animals could not survive in such cold conditions. But when greenhouse gases become too abundant, the resulting rising temperatures affect human health, livelihoods, and even threaten survival.

THE INDUSTRIAL REVOLUTION

For hundreds of years, the amount of CO_2 held steady at about 270 to 280 molecules for every million molecules of air. This is usually expressed as 270 to 280 ppm (parts per million). The numbers began to change with the start of the Industrial Revolution in the nineteenth century. Steam engines burned coal and oil to power factories. New machines took over jobs formerly done by hand. Although this led to a great increase in manufactured goods, the price to pay was pollution.

Coal, oil, and natural gas are called fossil fuels because they were formed over eons from the remains of prehistoric plants and trees. Since carbon is the basis of all life, these fuels also store carbon. When coal, oil, or natural gas is burned, carbon combines with oxygen to form CO_2. Since the start of the Industrial Revolution, power plants and the transportation industries have discharged billions of tons of greenhouse gases into the atmosphere.

Electricity and energy production account for more than 25 percent of global carbon emissions. This is almost double the emissions from the transportation industry. Coal-powered plants, like this one in Bełchatów, Poland, count for more than 65 percent of those emissions.

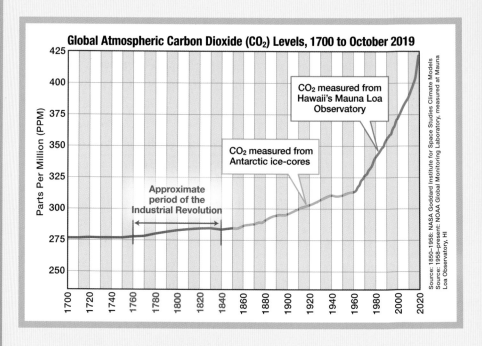

Global Atmospheric Carbon Dioxide (CO_2) Levels, 1700 to October 2019

Y-axis: Parts Per Million (PPM) — 250, 275, 300, 325, 350, 375, 400, 425

X-axis: 1700, 1720, 1740, 1760, 1780, 1800, 1820, 1840, 1860, 1880, 1900, 1920, 1940, 1960, 1980, 2000, 2020

CO_2 measured from Hawaii's Mauna Loa Observatory

CO_2 measured from Antarctic ice-cores

Approximate period of the Industrial Revolution

Source: 1850–1958: NASA Goddard Institute for Space Studies Climate Models
Source: 1958–present: NOAA Global Monitoring Laboratory, measured at Mauna Loa Observatory, HI

EXTREME CONDITIONS

The warming is taking a severe toll on Earth's ecological balances and weather patterns. Increasingly severe hurricanes, floods, heat waves, wild fires, and droughts provoke humanitarian crises throughout the world. The years from 2010-2019 saw extreme temperatures sweep the globe, making it the hottest decade on record. July 2019, the worst month, brought overwhelming hardship to western Europe. Hundreds died as extreme heat waves oppressed France, Belgium, Germany, the Netherlands, and England. Paris saw temperatures soar to 108.7°F (42.6°C).

Parched conditions and unprecedented heat set the stage for a surge in wildfires across the globe. More than eight thousand people were forced to flee raging wildfires in the Canary Islands off the northwest coast of Africa. The Amazon rain forest and the western United States also suffered devastating fires. Smoke was so widespread and dense that it could even be seen in satellite images taken from outer space. Areas of Greenland usually covered with snow burned out of control, spewing massive amounts of carbon dioxide into the air. In December 2019 and January 2020, Australia lost more than 25 million acres (10 million ha) to catastrophic wildfires that killed more than two dozen people and millions of animals. Damages ran into the billions. The devastation was so enormous that David Bowman, director of the Fire Centre Research Hub at the University of Tasmania, likened the fires to a "war situation."

At the opposite end of the weather spectrum, increasing temperatures enable the atmosphere to hold more water. This allows storms to produce heavier rainfalls. In 2019 Cyclone Idai killed more than one thousand people in southern Africa. Cyclone Fani pounded Bangladesh and India in May, causing 3.4 million people to evacuate their homes. Floods wreaked havoc in the southern and midwestern United States. Record rainfalls caused severe flooding in Iran during March and April. Six months later, Tokyo faced its worst storm in a decade. At least three people died, and dozens were injured. "This

DEFINING THE TERMS

Global warming, often in the news, is sometimes confused with climate change. Global warming refers to the gradual rise of temperatures across Earth over a long period of time. Climate change includes more than the actual warming of the planet. It also refers to the consequences of that warming, such as melting glaciers and sea ice, rising sea levels, and extreme weather events.

The relationship between climate and weather is also sometimes misunderstood. Weather is a short-time phenomenon that varies from day to day, sometimes drastically. Climate is a broader term that covers the average weather over a period of about thirty years. Traditionally, climate has referred to a specific location, such as the climate of northern Asia or the climate of the southwestern United States. But climate change, as experienced in the twenty-first century, refers to shifts in weather patterns all over the world.

ARE WE LIVING IN THE ANTHROPOCENE?

The Anthropocene has not been officially recognized as a geological epoch, but scientists have commonly used the term since 2000. Taken together, the two parts of the word, "anthropo" (man) and "cene" (new), stress that new, man-made forces are transforming Earth. Although many people believe that the advent of the Industrial Age in the nineteenth century should signify the start of the new era, others see the detonation of the first atomic bomb in 1945 as a more fitting beginning. Will Steffen, head of the Climate Change Institute at Australia National University, believes that when the Anthropocene started is not as important as what it conveys: "[It] will be another strong reminder to the general public that we are now having undeniable impacts on the environment at the scale of the planet as a whole, so much so that a new geological epoch has begun."

is the face of climate change," renowned climate scientist Michael Mann had said a year earlier, referring to the ominous worldwide scene. "We literally have not seen these extremes in the absence of climate change."

HOTHOUSE EARTH

Scientists agree that it is vital to lower carbon emissions if we are to preserve the planet and the conditions that sustain life for future generations. But will this be enough to stop the advance of climate change? Perhaps not, according to a report published in 2018 by the National Academy of Sciences. The sixteen authors of "Trajectories of the Earth System in the Anthropocene" (hereafter referred to as the "Trajectories" paper) did not break any new ground in their paper, but they took a detailed and sobering look at all the climate data to date. As the title indicates, their paper covers possible pathways (trajectories) that Earth's climate system could follow in a new geological period, the Anthropocene, one that has been created by human activity. The authors begin by posing four urgent questions:

1. IS THERE A THRESHOLD (SPECIFIC RISE IN GLOBAL TEMPERATURE) BEYOND WHICH CLIMATE CHANGE WILL ACCELERATE TOO RAPIDLY FOR HUMANITY TO STOP IT?
2. IF SO, WHAT IS THE THRESHOLD?
3. HOW WOULD CROSSING THIS THRESHOLD AFFECT HUMAN WELL-BEING?
4. WHAT CAN WE DO TO PREVENT EARTH FROM REACHING THE THRESHOLD?

The authors feel that Earth is changing much more rapidly than anyone expected or than at any time in past geological eras. If it keeps on its present course, the world may well cross a tipping point that triggers a

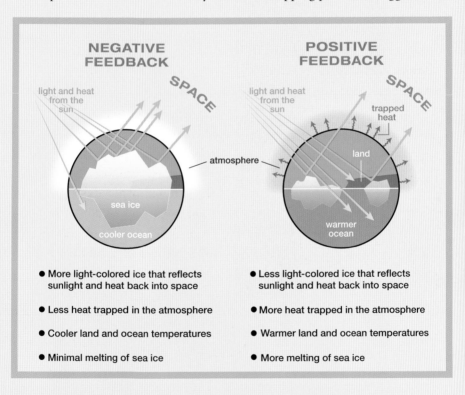

NEGATIVE FEEDBACK

light and heat from the sun

SPACE

atmosphere

sea ice

cooler ocean

POSITIVE FEEDBACK

light and heat from the sun

trapped heat

SPACE

land

warmer ocean

- More light-colored ice that reflects sunlight and heat back into space

- Less heat trapped in the atmosphere

- Cooler land and ocean temperatures

- Minimal melting of sea ice

- Less light-colored ice that reflects sunlight and heat back into space

- More heat trapped in the atmosphere

- Warmer land and ocean temperatures

- More melting of sea ice

series of runaway feedback loops to spiral out of control. Melting sea ice provides a vivid example. Because ice is light colored, it reflects a great deal of sunlight back into space, thus minimizing heat retention in the atmosphere. This is a *negative feedback* and counters the effects of climate change. As temperatures rise, however, ice begins to melt, exposing large dark regions of water or land. Dark areas absorb more light and heat than they reflect. Not only does this contribute to more warming, but it also leads to more ice melting. Then the expanded dark areas of Earth's surface absorb further sunlight, accelerating the loss of still more ice in a runaway *positive feedback*. As this example shows, positive feedbacks speed up the rate of global warming.

The longer they go unchecked, the more momentum positive feedbacks build up. "Once one [positive feedback, or tipping element] is pushed over, it pushes Earth towards another," explained Johan Rockström, one of the report's authors and former director of the Stockholm Resilience Centre, a research group dedicated to environmental issues. "It may be very difficult or impossible to stop the whole row of dominoes from tumbling over."

In such a scenario, known as hothouse Earth, global temperatures would reach heights not seen for 1.2 million years. Rising sea levels would submerge coastal cities, warming waters would destroy coral reefs, and large areas of land would become inhospitable to life. Not only would human health be endangered, but civilization could be at risk.

POINT OF NO RETURN

Rockström and his coauthors think that the point of no return could be an average global temperature rise of 3.6°F (2°C) over preindustrial times. But it's possible the threshold for runaway climate change may be even lower. Already the world temperature has increased 1.8°F (1°C) since the onset of the Industrial Revolution. A dozen US federal agencies predict that global temperatures could rise by at least 3°F (1.7°C) by the end of 2100 unless CO_2 emissions are drastically

THE WORDS REPORTERS USE MATTER

To many people, the term *climate change* is too bland. It doesn't convey the urgency of the global catastrophe already unfolding—how the world is changing or why. Atmospheric scientist Katharine Hayhoe used the more descriptive phrase "global weirding" in her web series about what is happening to our environment. In May 2019, the *Guardian* announced that it would no longer use the phrase "climate change." Instead, it would cover the "climate emergency, crisis, or breakdown." A number of other publications followed its lead. In June of the same year, Public Citizen, a nonprofit think tank based in Washington, DC, sent a letter to the presidents and CEOs of the major television networks, reminding them that "the words your reporters and anchors use matter. What they call something shapes how millions see it—and how entire nations act." the letter urged the networks to "call the climate crisis transforming the Earth exactly what it is: a climate crisis." A number of environmental groups, including Greenpeace, the Sunrise Movement, and the Sierra Club signed the letter.

reduced. "We have been pushing our planet to the brink and the damage is becoming increasingly clear," says the 2018 Global Risks Report from the World Economic Forum. This study predicts that severe weather will disrupt agriculture and cause a food shortage throughout the world. Insects that contribute to good crop yields may decrease in numbers, exacerbating the crisis. The report further reveals that weather disasters drove about 23.6 million people worldwide from their homes in 2016.

HOPE FOR THE FUTURE

Despite the alarming weather and dire expectations, scientists tell us that the technology already exists to curb climate change and

EARTHRISE

On Christmas Eve 1968, three astronauts circled the moon. In the midst of their activities, lunar module pilot Bill Anders glanced out the window. "Here's the earth coming up!" he cried. "Wow, is that pretty!" Anders was the official photographer for the Apollo 8 mission. Grabbing his camera, he quickly inserted a roll of color film and began taking pictures. His efforts resulted in the famous photograph, *Earthrise*, which NASA released in early 1969. The awe-inspiring blue-and-white globe suspended in space above the moon's featureless landscape captivated people all over the world. "People realized that we lived on this fragile planet and that we needed to take care of it," Anders recalled later.

Earthrise is one of the most reproduced space photographs of all time. It was named in *Life Magazine*'s 100 Photographs That Changed the World as "the most influential environmental photograph ever taken." The image shows parts of North and South America and Africa on Earth's surface.

The photograph is often credited with helping to inspire the first Earth Day on April 22, 1970, and giving fresh inspiration to the emerging environmental movement. Within a few years, Congress passed landmark legislation including the Clean Water Act (to lessen pollutants in lakes, rivers, and wetlands), the Clean Air Act (to minimize air pollution), and the National Environmental Policy Act (to preserve Earth's ecosystems). More than fifty years after the publication of *Earthrise*, many people hope the iconic photo will again inspire humanity to cherish Earth and do everything possible to preserve its beauty and ecological balances.

to protect the environment that supports human life. For example, alternative energy sources such as solar and wind power do not pollute the environment and are gaining in popularity. Techniques to suck CO_2 out of the atmosphere are being tested with great promise. Solar geoengineering, the manipulation of environmental processes to block sunlight from warming Earth, may also offer hope. But these techniques are highly controversial.

The authors of the "Trajectories" paper believe all of these measures have a role in combating climate change. But much more needs to be done at both the grassroots and global levels. Citizens of developed nations such as the United States must find ways to decrease their carbon footprints by reducing the amount of carbon their activities release into the atmosphere. Governments will have to reconsider social, political, and economic priorities to achieve a stabilized Earth and to assure the future of civilization. Radical changes in human behavior will be required to avoid irreversible changes to the environment.

CHAPTER TWO

HOTHOUSE EARTH

The crew of the US icebreaker *Nathaniel B. Palmer* huddled on the ship's bridge in the early morning hours. An enormous wall of ice loomed before them on the coast of western Antarctica. The immensity and almost other-worldly beauty of the Thwaites Glacier was breathtaking. But it hid a dangerous secret, revealed only by NASA's ice-penetrating radar. An enormous hole had opened underneath the glacier. About two-thirds the size of Manhattan, it could have held 14 billion tons (13 billion t) of ice.

Much of that ice had melted between 2016 and 2019 in an accelerating positive feedback. This is what is happening. As more water and warmth accumulate in the hole underneath the ice, more melting takes place. This increases the size of the hole, making space for even more warm water to infiltrate the underside of the glacier. Then the extra water speeds up the melting, allowing for still more warm water to enter the hole in a cycle spiraling out of control.

As participants in a five-year study by the United States and the United Kingdom, the crew of the *Palmer* expedition was investigating the ice, collecting data in front of, above, and underneath the glacier. Researchers will use all the evidence to determine how Thwaites behaved in the past and to predict the extent of future melting. Scientists worry that if Thwaites were to collapse, nearby glaciers might also weaken, eventually causing seas to rise as much as 11 feet (3.4 m). But they don't know how long it would take. "How much? How fast? That's our mantra," said Robert Larter, a scientist aboard the *Palmer*, said in January 2019. Just a year later, scientists announced

The Thwaites Glacier has shown signs of rapid decay in the past few years with a vast cavity opening beneath it. The loss of the Thwaites Glacier would allow more sections of the Antarctic ice sheet to give way, leading to a dangerous rise in sea level.

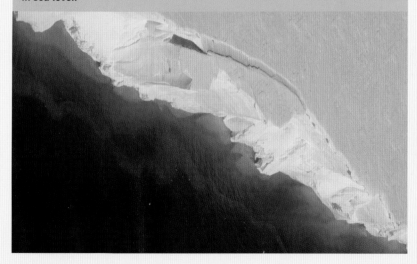

the discovery of warm water at an especially critical location beneath Thwaites. They fear this may signal an irreversible shrinking.

POSITIVE FEEDBACKS

Scientists are asking those same questions about climate change in general as they are about Thwaites. How much should we expect temperatures, ecological balances, and the environment to change? How fast might we expect these changes to happen? The authors of the "Trajectories" paper say that the answers depend on the number of positive feedbacks triggered by the amount of CO_2 in the atmosphere. If tipping points (also called tipping cascades) are reached and positive feedbacks take over, it is difficult to predict how rapidly sea levels might rise, hurricanes intensify, or heat waves and droughts increase. Will Steffen, Johan Rockström, and their coauthors assert that what humans do in the next one or two decades could "significantly" affect Earth for up to hundreds of thousands of years. They say that human activity could "potentially lead to conditions that resemble planetary states that were last seen several millions of years ago, conditions that would be hostile to human societies and to many other contemporary species."

No one can say exactly how many positive feedbacks exist. New ones are still being discovered. Especially significant ones include the following:

Water vapor. Warmer air holds more water vapor than colder air. So when temperatures rise, larger amounts of water evaporate from lakes, seas, and other bodies of water. This becomes water vapor in the atmosphere. Since water vapor is also a greenhouse gas, it traps heat in the atmosphere. So rising CO_2 levels lead to warmer temperatures. And they lead to more water vapor in the air, causing still more warming in a positive feedback loop.

Ice albedo. Another basic feedback concerns polar ice. As we have seen in the first chapter, ice reflects sunlight back into space and

GREENLAND ICE SHEET

Greenland's vast ice sheet is in serious jeopardy. A study published in January 2019 in the *Proceedings of the National Academy of Sciences* suggests that the ice sheet may already have hit a tipping point that has greatly accelerated its melting. Between 2002 and 2016, about 280 billion tons (254 billion t) of ice disappeared each year. It's difficult to visualize such an amount. But if you imagine New York and Florida submerged in 2 to 3 feet (0.6 to 0.9 m) of water with enough water left over to flood Washington, DC, and one or two additional smaller states, you will have an idea of Greenland's annual ice loss. Even at this mind-boggling rate, it would take centuries for the ice sheet to melt completely. But if the global temperature continues to rise in the next few years or decades, there could be no stopping its complete disappearance.

On a smaller timescale, the meltwater contributes to rises in sea levels and may be interfering with the Gulf Stream. A warm ocean current originating around the equator, the Gulf Stream brings moderate temperatures to northern latitudes, including western Europe. Meltwater from Greenland slows down the Gulf Stream and may have helped cause the devastating heat waves and wildfires that struck Europe in the summer of 2019.

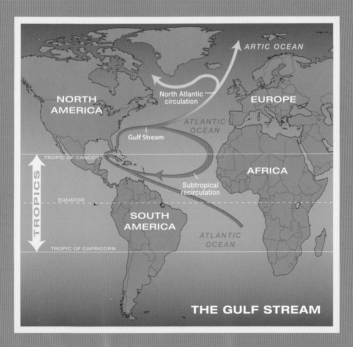

THE GULF STREAM

thereby causes a cooling effect. The amount of light reflected by a surface is its albedo. When ice melts, dark land or water is exposed that lessens its albedo, absorbs heat, and increases the temperature.

Wildfires. Occasional wildfires have always existed and, in many instances, benefit the land. By burning accumulated leaves, rotting wood, and tangled bushes, fires release nutrients and minerals into the soil and clear the ground for new growth. But recent mega-fires have wreaked massive destruction and provoked widespread panic as people and animals flee the towering infernos. On the rise throughout the world, wildfires burned over 10 million acres (4 million ha) in the United States alone in 2017. Two years later, from early September 2019 through early January 2020, the world watched in shock and horror as fires in Australia devastated more than 26 million acres (10.5 million ha). As vast numbers of trees and plants burn, they release large amounts of CO_2 into the air. The Australian fires discharged an estimated 400 million tons (363 million t) of CO_2 into the air. This is about equal to the United Kingdom's output for a whole year. This additional carbon dioxide contributes to further warming, and that increases the risk of more wildfires.

Ashes and smoke from fires also harm the environment. The Australian fires created a massive trail of soot and smoke that circled the globe. Dark soot landing on snow and ice reduces the albedo effect, holding more heat on Earth and allowing less heat to escape into space. In addition, soot and smoke can accelerate the melting of glaciers. The loss of life and destruction of property as well as the potential for worldwide intensification of climate change make wildfire feedback one of the most feared.

Melting permafrost. Located mostly in the far north, permafrost is land that has been frozen for at least two years. Many areas, however, have been frozen for hundreds or even thousands of years. Permafrost ranges in depth from a few feet to more than 1 mile (1.6 km). Because the bodies of many plants and animals lie frozen in the permafrost,

Increased demand for dairy and beef products and soy feed for livestock has motivated extensive burning and clearing of the Amazon rain forest. During the dry season of 2019 (June–August), about 3,500 square miles (9,060 sq. km) were burned in forty thousand separate fires. This represents a 77 percent increase in the number of fires from 2018. The fires threaten the Amazon's biodiversity and indigenous inhabitants in addition to releasing carbon dioxide and monoxide into the atmosphere.

it contains huge amounts of carbon. When permafrost melts, microscopic organisms decompose the bodies, releasing vast amounts of carbon dioxide and methane (a greenhouse gas more potent than CO_2) into the air. It is believed that the top 10 feet (3 m) of the permafrost holds 1,700 metric gigatons of carbon, twice the amount present in the atmosphere in 2014. Scientists warn that the warming caused by the release of this carbon will activate a runaway feedback loop of more permafrost melting and more rising temperatures.

Amazon rain forest dieback. The world's largest tropical rain forest, the Amazon, is home to numerous species of plants and animals. Some of them are not found anywhere else in the world. Climate scientists are particularly worried about the effect El Niño has on this luxuriant ecological system. El Niño is a regularly occurring climate condition that may last from several months to two to three years. Although El Niño brings storms and extreme precipitation to some areas, it causes dry weather and drought in other areas. Such conditions are conducive to wildfires. The situation is especially dangerous because a great deal of the Amazon is deliberately burned to clear land for farming or mining. Although carefully monitored, these blazes can rage out of control, destroying much more tropical growth than intended. Apart from the danger of fire, trees do not grow as much in warm, dry weather, and so they store less carbon. All of this means more CO_2 in the air, more heat waves, more dieback (a situation where plants and trees begin to die from the tips of their roots or leaves). The dying leaves release still more CO_2 as the cycle repeats. Large areas of rain forest could be destroyed in this way.

CLIMATE CHANGE'S EVIL TWIN

Not all carbon dioxide released on Earth ends up in the atmosphere or stored in trees and vegetation. Almost 26 percent, or about 2.6 billion tons (2.4 billion t), a year of CO_2 dissolves in the ocean. In this way, oceans play a critical role in keeping air temperatures at lower levels and slowing down climate change. But some of the CO_2 interacts with water to form carbonic acid. This gradually increases the acidity of the ocean and interferes with the way marine creatures such as crabs, clams, oysters, and coral reefs build their shells and skeletons. As their numbers decline, a cascade of harmful consequences ensues. Larger species that feed on these animals cannot find food. The fishing industry suffers, as do millions of people who depend on seafood as their source of protein. Tiny plant and animal organisms that might have been used to develop new medicines are lost. And increasing acidification lessens the ocean's ability to absorb more CO_2. The additional CO_2 that stays in the atmosphere can only accelerate the warming and climate change. Not surprisingly, ocean acidification is sometimes labeled global warming's "evil twin."

CORAL REEFS

Coral reefs, found off the shorelines of tropical and subtropical waters, are among the best-known casualties of climate change and ocean acidification. They are remarkable structures consisting of tiny animals, or polyps, that live in partnership with simple aquatic plants, or algae. The algae provide nourishment for the polyps through photosynthesis. The algae use sunlight to convert water and CO_2 into food. Then the polyps emit the limestone that forms the skeleton or structure of the reefs. The algae produce the glorious colors for which the reefs are famous.

When healthy coral experiences environmental stress, such as high temperatures or acid levels, it ejects the algae that live inside it and appears white, or bleached. Bleached coral is not necessarily dead, but unless the environmental stressors disappear and the algae return, bleached coral will eventually die.

If waters become too warm, however, the algae may photosynthesize nutrients faster than the corals can manage. This causes the coral to eject the algae. Without the beautiful colors provided by the algae, the skeletal reefs turn white, a condition known as coral bleaching.

According to some studies, ocean acidification may pose an even greater risk to coral reefs than climate change. It hampers the ability of polyps to produce strong, sturdy reefs. It may also weaken existing reefs, making them more brittle and less able to withstand warming temperatures. These and other threats to coral reefs, such as water pollution and overfishing, also endanger the many thousands of species that depend on them. Then this jeopardizes as many as one billion people who depend on fish living around coral reefs as a source of food.

CLOUD APOCALYPSE?

Low-lying layers of thin, rounded stratocumulus clouds cover about a fifth of Earth's surface. Because they are especially good at reflecting heat from the sun back into space, they cool Earth better than most other clouds. They also provide a great deal of cooling shade. Based on computer models, a team of climate scientists at the California Institute of Technology (Caltech) speculate that rising CO_2 levels could change this in the distant future. At CO_2 concentrations of around 1,200 ppm (three times the current level), stratus clouds would dissipate, setting off what some call a "cloud apocalypse."

In this unproven but plausible scenario, the loss of stratocumulus clouds could cause tropical oceans to warm by 14°F (8°C) and subtropical waters to warm by 18°F (10°C) degrees. Warm-blooded animals would not be able to tolerate such temperatures. Tapio Schneider, the lead author of the Caltech study, believes "that technological changes will slow carbon emissions so that we do not actually reach such high CO_2 concentrations. But our results show that there are dangerous climate change thresholds that we have been unaware of."

PUSHING THE SYSTEM TOO FAR

Scientists fear that melting permafrost, forest dieback, ocean acidification, and other processes that are well underway could plunge the world into the hothouse Earth state. "We are now seeing signs that we are pushing the system (natural cycles of nature) too far," Rockström told the website Live Science in August 2018. "The moment the planet becomes a source of greenhouse gas emissions together with us humans, then as you can imagine, things are accelerating very fast in the wrong direction."

In a hothouse Earth scenario, average global temperatures would read 7°F to 9°F (4°C to 5°C) above preindustrial levels. Sea levels would loom 33 to 200 feet (10 to 60 m) higher, flooding vast areas of coastline. Floods, wildfires, and extreme storms would become more frequent and violent. Decline in crop yields would lead to widespread famine and vast numbers of refugees. Deadly conflicts would ensue over the rights to most habitable regions of the planet.

LOSS OF BIODIVERSITY

Meanwhile, plant and animal species are already dying off at an alarming rate. According to a UN report published in 2019, "Around 1 million species already face extinction, many within decades, unless action is taken." A number of factors account for the loss of biodiversity (a wide variety of life-forms). Farming practices, mining, overfishing, deforestation, water pollution, an increase in roads, and the growth of cities all contribute to the endangerment of species. Man-made climate change also alters the environment, making a frightening situation even worse. The report states that the survival of more than half a million land species, including many birds and insects, are threatened as their natural habitats dwindle.

Human health and well-being is greatly impacted by species extinction. More than 559 animal breeds raised by humans have already gone extinct. Another 1,000 are threatened. In many areas, pollinators (birds, bats, and especially insects and bees that move pollen from one part of a plant to another) are declining in number. But three-quarters of food crops depend on pollination. If pollinators were to become extinct, the world could suffer an annual loss of about $235 to $577 billion in food crops, and many people would go hungry.

Robert Watson, chair of the group that wrote the UN report, fears that effects of climate change on species extinction "are accelerating." He said in 2019 that "we cannot solve the threats of human-induced climate change and loss of biodiversity in isolation. We either solve both or we solve neither."

THE DIFFERENCE BETWEEN THE POSSIBLE AND THE IMPOSSIBLE

The fate of humanity depends not only on science but also on politics. Although Earth will never be as it was, solutions exist to lessen some of the worst effects of climate change. Researchers and environmentalists stress that it's up to governments to set priorities, enact legislation, and make funding available for the sweeping transformations that must take place and for the creation of jobs in new green industries. Stephen Cornelius is the chief adviser on climate change to the World Wide Fund for Nature. "We have the targets, we have the solutions," he said in 2018, "and the difference between the impossible and possible is political leadership."

CLIMATE SCIENCE PIONEERS

The names Eunice Foote and John Tyndall are not well known, but their work provides the foundation for climate crisis studies. In 1856, Foote showed that CO_2 holds heat. Three years later, Tyndall (unaware of Foote's work) came to the same conclusion. Both recognized that more CO_2 in the atmosphere would make the world warmer.

CLIMATE HERO CHARLES DAVID KEELING AND THE KEELING CURVE

Charles David Keeling enjoyed the outdoors, but his trip to Big Sur in 1955 wasn't just about camping out. He brought along special containers to store air from the popular state park. Aware of the growing use of fossil fuels, he wanted to know what effect this had on the amount of CO_2 in the air. Although other scientists had measured atmospheric CO_2 levels, Keeling developed a more efficient and accurate technique. His early measurements in California and other western states showed the background level of CO_2 to be 310 parts per million.

Keeling's work attracted the attention of a great many scientists, including Roger Revelle of the Scripps Institution of Oceanography in San Diego. Revelle wanted to take CO_2 measurements from many locations high in the atmosphere over a long period. He hired Keeling, and together, they set up a research station toward the top of Mauna Loa, a huge volcano on Hawaii. The remote site would allow them to obtain air that had not been polluted by emissions from large cities. They also collected air from high-flying weather balloons. Their measurements documented an alarming rise in CO_2 levels each year.

The findings also revealed a seasonal variation in atmospheric CO_2 due to photosynthesis. Photosynthesis is the complex process that allows plants, algae, and some forms of bacteria to pull CO_2 from the air. Using energy from the sun, plants combine molecules of water and CO_2 to produce glucose and release oxygen. As trees leaf out and flowers bloom in the spring, they take in carbon dioxide. This produces a measurable dip in atmospheric CO_2. In the fall, as plants and leaves die, carbon is released and atmospheric levels rise again. Some scientists view this annual cycle as Earth breathing. When CO_2 levels are plotted as a graph over time, they show the steady increase of a sawtooth (due to seasonal differences) pattern. This is known as the Keeling Curve.

CHAPTER THREE

SCIENTIFIC WARNINGS AND POLITICAL STRUGGLES

I n December 2007, NASA scientist and climate change expert James Hansen stood before the American Geophysical Union meeting in San Francisco. That summer the Arctic ice cover had shrunk to record lows as carbon emissions continued to rise. According to the National Oceanic and Atmospheric Administration, the CO_2 level already topped 383 ppm and showed no signs of leveling off. Many scientists wondered how much CO_2 the air could contain without seriously affecting our safety and well-being.

Hansen had a frightening answer to their question. Backing up his claim with a detailed analysis of recent data and climate studies of past geological ages, he declared the maximum safe level of atmospheric carbon dioxide to be 350 parts per million (350 ppm). The world had already crossed that dangerous threshold by over 30 ppm of CO_2. If Hansen was correct, climate change was more than a problem for future generations. Earth was already in serious trouble. In his book, *Eaarth*, environmentalist and writer Bill McKibben recalled Hansen's announcement as "the day I knew we'd never again inhabit the planet I'd been born on, or anything close to it." McKibben purposefully misspelled the word "earth" to distinguish between the planet that has sustained us and the planet toward which the climate change is rapidly propelling us.

LIKE A SPEEDING FREIGHT TRAIN

Despite Hansen's warning, carbon emissions have continued to increase, passing 400 ppm in 2013. By December 2019, they topped an alarming 411 ppm. Scientists have likened the accelerating pace to "a speeding freight train." The rising levels have been linked to extreme weather across the globe. Early 2019 saw Minnesota residents enduring temperatures of –58°F (–50°C) as weakening winds in the Arctic allowed

Although Minnesota is used to cold winters, polar vortices cause temperatures to drop to extreme levels. The weather is made even worse by wind chills of –40°F (–40°C). In these conditions, frostbite can develop on exposed skin in less than ten minutes.

freezing temperatures to move south. At least twenty-three people died. Severe cold waves also hit parts of England and Europe, disrupting airline flights and stranding motorists. At the opposite extreme, record high temperatures in Australia during the same time melted roads and caused thousands of animals and hundreds of thousands of fish to die.

THE POLAR VORTEX

Skeptics have sometimes pointed to cold spells to refute the existence of climate change. Can global warming and record-breaking cold temperatures both be true? they ask. Yes, say climate scientists. The Arctic is warming more rapidly than the rest of the planet. As sea ice melts, heat is released from the ocean. This heat weakens the polar vortex winds that circle high above the Arctic in the stratosphere. Cold air that is usually confined to the polar area escapes southward bringing dangerously low temperatures to northern Europe and Russia. "This trend can explain most of the cooling of Eurasian winters since 1990," Marlene Kretschmer of the Potsdam Institute for Climate Impact Research said in 2017.

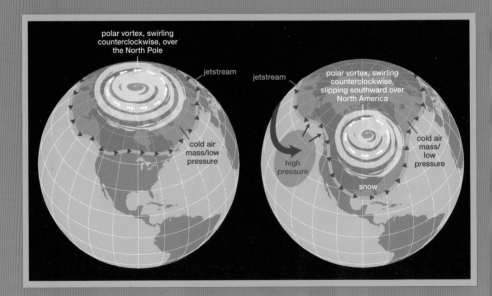

The year 2020 continued the trend toward higher temperatures. Global temperatures in May were the highest ever recorded, including in the famously cold region of Siberia. The Russian town of Verkhoyansk, located above the Arctic Circle, registered 100.4°F (38°C) on June 20. Danish climate scientist Martin Stendel attributes the unprecedented heat to human activity. Without climate change, he said, "there is a 1 in 100,000 chance of such a hot May in [Siberia]. It's virtually impossible."

Climate experts predict dire circumstances for much of the world after the year 2050. As up to 44 percent of the world's landmass becomes parched, droughts will occur in North America, southern Europe, and much of Southeast Asia and South America. And excessive rainfall will cause floods on other parts of the planet, risking the safety and homes of two billion people. Scientists say there is a 10 to 30 percent chance that the world's most populated areas could experience temperatures above 130°F (55°C) by 2100.

CLIMATE MIGRANTS

Excessive heat, dry spells, and droughts are expected to cause crop failures and critical food shortages throughout the world. Even as food prices rise, extreme temperatures are expected to lower the nutritional content of surviving crops. Violent conflicts will increase as rival populations fight to secure the most fertile land or best source of water. Herders too will

Many refugee camps struggle with overcrowding, and the Moria refugee camp in Lesbos, Greece, is no different. Without enough room or resources for all the migrants, some are forced to sleep in summer tents despite rain and cold weather.

have to compete for the best places to graze their animals as grasslands wither and die. Ultimately, poverty and violence could force millions from their homes to seek resources and safety in an increasingly hazardous world. The migrations have already started. One example involves the drought in Syria between 2006 and 2011. Many experts believe the hunger and suffering that the Syrian people endured contributed to the ensuing civil war. More than eleven million Syrians were displaced, six million of them within their own country.

The migrant caravan that pushed forward through Mexico to the US border at San Diego in October 2018 is another example. Members of the caravan sought asylum because they were targeted by gangs in Central American cities. But many of them had come to those cities because of poor crop harvests. They were no longer able to eke out a living as farmers. "The main reason people are moving is because they don't have anything to eat," Robert Albro of the Center for Latin American and Latino Studies at American University said. "This (migrant caravan) has a strong link to climate change—we are seeing tremendous climate instability that is radically changing food security in the region."

INNOCENT VICTIMS

Like Constance Okollet and the people of Uganda, many of those suffering the worst effects of climate change come from underdeveloped nations that have contributed little to the world's rising carbon emissions. About 1.3 billion people in the world live without electricity. This is particularly true in parts of Africa, Asia, and South America. These countries have done almost nothing to further climate change, yet the safety and livelihood of their citizens are most at risk. Often these countries are in warm or low-lying areas that are prone to severe weather. Compounding the problem, their governments lack the funds to prepare for or recover from weather disasters. World leaders realize that the energy and health needs of these people must be met at the same time the world strives to lower carbon emissions.

THE KYOTO PROTOCOL

Recognizing the need for global action, the United Nations created the Framework Convention on Climate Change at the Earth Summit in Rio de Janeiro, Brazil, in 1992. Almost every nation signed this treaty that committed them to keep greenhouse gas concentrations "at a level that would prevent dangerous anthropogenic (human-induced) interference with the climate system." But the details of how to accomplish this were left up to individual countries. Something more was needed to bind the international community together in a stronger way. Under the Kyoto Protocol, signed five years later in December

THE MOST CONSEQUENTIAL LIE IN HUMAN HISTORY

By the late 1970s, oil companies such as Exxon knew that CO_2 emissions posed a serious environmental crisis. Instead of publicizing their findings, they launched a campaign to "emphasize the uncertainty" of climate science—even though no uncertainty existed. Writer and environmentalist Bill McKibben has called this "the most consequential lie in human history." As the idea of climate change became more familiar to the public, Exxon financed organizations to create the false impression that scientists were divided on the topic. Exxon worked with the National Coal Association and the American Petroleum Institute to fight a tax that had been proposed on fossil fuels. Taking advantage of the melting Arctic ice that made drilling possible, Exxon made a $500 billion deal to seek oil in the northern regions of Russia. Though financially beneficial to the company, the move would certainly contribute to climate change. The company also stirred up opposition to the 1997 Kyoto Protocol, the first international treaty calling on nations to reduce carbon emissions. The dishonesty of the oil companies helped confuse the American public, fostering an attitude of climate denial and delaying critical action to curb greenhouse gases.

THE DIFFERENCE OF A HALF DEGREE

The Paris Agreement of 2015 aims to limit average global temperatures to "well below 2 degrees C [3.6°F] above pre-industrial levels," but it encourages countries to strive for a temperature increase of only 2.7°F (1.5°C). Although it may seem like a slight difference, a great deal hangs on that 0.9°F (0.5°C). According to a study published by the European Geosciences Union in April 2016, heat waves would be about one-third longer and storms would be about one-third stronger with an extra half-degree temperature rise. Sea levels would rise by a third. For coral reefs, the outlook is grimmer. With a 2°C increase, coral reefs would vanish by 2100.

The 0.5°C (0.9°F) increase would make a huge difference in the yields of some crops. This is because the temperature rise might not hold steady throughout the year. For a short period (perhaps several weeks or months), a region could be considerably warmer. The rest of the year would be cooler. When the temperature rise for the whole year is averaged, it would only come out to 1.5° or 2°C (2.7° or 3.6°F) warmer. But if the extra high temperatures come during an important point in the plants' development, the crops would be severely damaged. For example, corn might survive, but it wouldn't produce seeds. All combined, the effects of the half-degree rise in temperatures would be disastrous to humanity. According to the United Nation's Intergovernmental Panel on Climate Change (IPCC) report in 2018, the additional half degree of warming between 1.5° and 2°C would put hundreds of millions more people's lives in danger.

1997, industrialized nations pledged to lower their annual emissions of greenhouse gases by various amounts. Underdeveloped countries, whose emissions were a mere fraction of the emissions of wealthier nations, were not required to decrease their emissions. The United States never ratified the treaty, which went into effect in 2005, possibly due to fears that the treaty would hurt the economy.

THE PARIS AGREEMENT: A POWERFUL SIGNAL

Security was tight when leaders and delegates from almost two hundred countries came together for UN climate talks in Paris in 2015. The previous month a series of terrorist attacks had shocked and frightened the city. One hundred thirty-two people died in the attacks, as well as nine of the eleven terrorists. Hundreds were injured at six different locations. Concerned that a large international gathering might prompt further attacks, some people argued that the conference should be canceled, but the president of France, François Hollande, was adamant that talks go forward.

In July 2019, France experienced a powerful heat wave that closed schools and sent people flocking to public water fountains. Temperatures were in excess of 100°F (38°C), breaking several of the country's previous temperature records.

Tensions ran high for another reason. The Kyoto Protocol had failed to lower global carbon emissions. By 2011 China and the United States were releasing enough greenhouse gases to negate any progress made by other countries. UN meetings throughout the ten years following Kyoto had been filled with dissension and had not produced a strong, workable treaty. Global temperatures were forecast to rise as much as 9°F (5°C) with disastrous results. The leaders were desperate to come up with a workable agreement. But serious differences continued to divide them—especially the question of financial help to developing countries that suffered severe weather

KEN SMITH: HOW ARE WE GOING TO PROVIDE FOR OUR FAMILIES?

No one expected Ken Smith to stand up and introduce himself at the UN Climate Change Conference in Paris in 2015. An oil sands mechanic from Canada, he depended on fossil fuels for his living. As president of his local union chapter in Alberta, he represented thirty-five hundred oil workers. "We hope we are seeing the end of fossil fuels for the good of everybody," Smith said. "But how are we going to provide for our families?" His spontaneous words stunned his listeners. "We're going to need some kind of transition," Smith continued. "The scientists are saying [global warming] is not a fantasy, the fire is at our heels. So I'm asking everyone at this convention, help us build those bridges [to new jobs in sustainable areas]. We want to be full partners because we have no choice." The audience appreciated his honesty—both about the climate crisis and his livelihood. When Smith sat down, they gave him a standing ovation.

Many Canadian officials believe that the future, while difficult, will offer more jobs in renewable energy. "The good news is that lots of the skills needed to work in the oil sands are going to be useful with clean energy," said Merran Smith, executive director of Clean Energy Canada. "Electricians, welding, carpenters, engineers and more."

events linked to climate change. The outcome of the conference remained in doubt until its very end. When an agreement was finally announced, thousands of delegates broke into applause and cheers.

The deal aimed to prevent global temperatures from rising 3.6°F (2°C) above preindustrial levels, but it encouraged countries to work toward limiting the rise to 2.7°F (1.5°C). To meet this goal, both industrialized and developing nations would be required to drastically reduce greenhouse gas emissions. The agreement included an article on loss and damages that provided funds to help poor countries overcome climate disasters and to transition to renewable energy sources.

Speaking from the White House, President Barack Obama hailed the Paris Agreement "as a powerful signal that the world is fully committed to a low-carbon future. We've shown that the world has both the will and the ability to take on this challenge."

United Nations secretary-general Ban Ki-moon also praised the treaty as "a truly universal agreement on climate change." Signed April 22, 2016, the Paris Agreement went into effect on November 4, 2016.

US WITHDRAWAL

But less than one year later, President Donald Trump announced plans to withdraw the United States from the Paris Agreement. The move distressed many people throughout the world, including members of his own staff. The agreement had obligated the US to reduce carbon emissions by 26 to 28 percent below 2005 levels by 2025. The country was also supposed to help underdeveloped nations with up to $3 billion by 2020. Trump declared that he wanted a better deal for the United States. "I was elected to represent the citizens of Pittsburgh, not Paris," he said.

Pittsburgh's mayor, Bill Peduto, replied in an indignant tweet, "I can assure you that we will follow the guidelines of the Paris Agreement for our people, our economy & future."

Across the country, governors, mayors, college presidents, and business leaders pledged to uphold the agreement despite Trump's withdrawal. "We're going to do everything America would have done if it had stayed committed," said former New York mayor Michael Bloomberg.

Elon Musk, founder of the Tesla car company, predicted that Trump's action would hurt the economy. Obama agreed, saying, "The nations that remain in the Paris agreement will be the nations that reap the benefits in jobs and industries created."

ATTRIBUTION SCIENCE

Many people wonder about the relationship between severe weather and climate change. How can scientists say that a particular storm or a wildfire was due to climate change? The answer lies in the rapidly developing field of extreme event attribution.

As recently as 2003, most scientists assumed that it was impossible to calculate how climate change affected any particular weather event. Climate expert Myles Allen wondered about that, however. "Everybody was saying, 'Well, you can't attribute a single event to climate change,'" he said. "And this prompted me to ask, 'Why not?'"

The next year Allen, colleague Daithi Stone, and Peter Stott of the UK's Meteorological Office published a paper that investigated the way in which climate impacted a 2003 heat wave in Europe that caused tens of thousands of deaths. Building on previous science, the paper discussed two kinds of computer simulations—those that took human-induced rising levels of CO_2 and rising temperatures into account and those that did not factor climate change into the results. According to the authors' assessment, climate change more or less doubled the chance of a particular heat wave occurring.

As interest grew in attribution science, more and more papers were published. Scientists stress that a number of factors influence the development of a specific weather event. For this reason, no one can prove that climate change is the sole reason for any individual cyclone or drought. But scientists can determine the extent to which climate change influenced the likelihood of a particular event. And they can assess the degree to which climate change increased the severity.

ALARMING CLIMATE ASSESSMENTS

Scientists continue to warn that time is running out for humanity to reverse climate change. The highly publicized "Trajectories" paper published in August 2018 was followed by a report from the IPCC that was presented in Korea on October 5. The report, by 91 lead authors and 133 contributing authors, included alarming statistics. According to the UN, human activities such as manufacturing, transportation, and energy usage release 42 billion tons (38 billion t) of carbon dioxide into the atmosphere each year. At this rate, the world will experience temperature increases of 5.4°F to 7.2°F (3°C to 4°C)—well above the safety limit set by the Paris Agreement.

On the heels of the IPCC report came an equally disturbing report of over sixteen hundred pages issued by the US government in November. Experts found that by the end of the twenty-first century, the US economy could lose hundreds of billions of dollars if greenhouse gas emissions aren't significantly lessened. Damage would include lower crop yields and reduced hauls for the fishing industry. Coastal flooding could wreak billions of dollars of damages to homes, businesses, roads, bridges, and transportation systems. Torrential rains could disrupt sewage systems, causing contaminated water to pour into rivers.

The report predicted an increase in health problems across the nation. Excessive heat could lead to dehydration, heatstroke, and worsening of heart conditions. Disease-bearing insects can flourish in warmer climates, expanding their natural habitat and causing more cases of illnesses such as Lyme disease or West Nile virus. The risk of new diseases and possible pandemics becomes greater from closer human contact with other species.

Climate change will also make air pollution worse because warmer air can hold greater numbers of aerosols, tiny droplets or solid particles that come from car exhausts, factory emissions, wildfires, plant pollens, or other natural or man-made sources. People with respiratory ailments such as asthma, bronchitis, or chronic obstructive pulmonary disease (COPD) will experience a worsening of symptoms. Children, the elderly, and those living in low-income areas face the greatest danger. The report ends on an understated but sobering note: "The assumption that current and future climate conditions will resemble the recent past is no longer valid."

TRUMP'S DENIAL

The UN and US reports stand in stark contrast to Trump's continued denials of climate change. Some observers felt the report's release date, the Friday after Thanksgiving, was a deliberate attempt to lessen its impact. Caught up in the holiday weekend, many people might miss the report or pay little attention to it.

A spokesperson for the White House said that the report was "largely based on the most extreme scenario," and ignored the possibility of new insights and technological insights.

Katharine Hayhoe, a climate scientist at Texas Tech University, dismissed the White House claim as "demonstrably false." On Twitter, she explained that she had written the chapter on climate scenarios that includes all possible developments "from those where we go carbon negative before end of century to those where carbon emissions continue to rise."

GREEN NEW DEAL

In November 2018, several hundred young people squeezed into US House representative Nancy Pelosi's office in Washington, DC. The members of the Sunrise Movement had come to demand action on climate change and to enlist the support of the woman likely to become the next Speaker of the House of Representatives. Newly elected representative Alexandria Ocasio-Cortez, a New York Democrat and the youngest congresswoman-elect in US history, joined the protest. During her campaign, she had spoken forcefully in favor of a Green New Deal (named after President Franklin Roosevelt's New Deal policy to boost the US economy in the 1930s). It would combine climate action with economic growth and social justice.

On February 7, 2019, Ocasio-Cortez introduced the Green New Deal into Congress as a nonbinding resolution calling on the government to transition from fossil fuels to 100 percent renewable energy. Such a move would create many high-salaried jobs in renewable energy, thereby boosting the economy, she claimed. The document included sweeping demands: a smart grid able to distribute electricity with little or no waste, renovations of buildings to become energy efficient, decarbonization of agriculture and factories, carbon-free transportation and repair of infrastructure, and investments in technology to remove CO_2 from the atmosphere.

New York representative Alexandria Ocasio-Cortez rallies for the Green New Deal proposal on November 14, 2019, in Washington, DC. She was joined by presidential candidate Senator Bernie Sanders, affordable housing advocates, and climate change activists for her announcement. In addition to pushing for lower carbon emissions, the Green New Deal addressed the housing crisis in America by planning for new cheaper housing developments across the country.

Supporters believe an intense focus on green technology would make the United States a global leader in the production of clean energy, a model that other countries could emulate.

Less than two months later, the Senate, voting along party lines, defeated the resolution. But the idea continues to gain traction. In June 2020, Democrats in the House of Representatives released a Climate Crisis Action Plan incorporating many ideas from the Green New Deal. Calling for net-zero carbon emissions by 2050, the plan links climate solutions to social justice, racial equality, and humanitarian concerns. The report calls on the United States to "harness the technological innovation of the moonshot, the creativity of our entrepreneurs, the strength of our workers, and the moral force of a nation endeavoring to establish justice for all."

COP25: THE POINT OF NO RETURN

Striking out independently of the Trump administration, US congressional leader Nancy Pelosi led a group of fifteen congresspersons to the twenty-fifth UN Conference on Climate Change (called the Conference of the Parties, or COP25) that met in Madrid, Spain, in December 2019. She spoke of numerous cities and states committed to the Paris Agreement despite the official withdrawal of the United States. "We're here to say to all of you, on behalf of the House of Representatives and the Congress of the United States, we're still in it, we're still in it," Pelosi told the thousands of delegates from all over the world.

UN secretary-general António Guterres underscored the urgency of the proceedings by predicting a climate change "point-of-no-return" that is "in sight and hurtling towards us." "Do we really want to be remembered as the generation that buried its head in the sand, that fiddled while the planet burned?" he asked.

The next two weeks proved contentious. The conference did make some progress with seventy-three nations, responsible for 10 percent of the world's carbon emissions, pledging to expand their climate change programs. Positive news also came from the European Union, which declared its intention to become carbon neutral by 2050. Many local areas, including cities and businesses, are working toward that same goal—the elimination of all carbon emissions by the middle of the century. But according to many participants and observers, this was not nearly enough. No global agreement was reached on how to handle the devastation wrought by man-made climate change and how to finance ways to minimize the destruction of future events. Many people felt the final document did not live up to the commitments set forth in the 2015 Paris Agreement. Neil Thorns, advocacy director for the Catholic Agency for Overseas Development (CAFOD), released a statement that summed up the general dissatisfaction: "It's unbelievable when we've seen people worldwide calling urgently, loudly and ever more desperately for action that the negotiators at the COP in Madrid have responded so meekly."

YOUTH MOVEMENT: WE ARE UNSTOPPABLE

Youth activists were especially disappointed in the outcome of COP25. The 2019 conference marked the first time that members of the youth climate movement, a rapidly growing phenomenon, attended in large numbers. "Finding holistic solutions is what the COP should be all about," said sixteen-year-old youth activist and founder of the School Strikes for Climate Change Movement Greta Thunberg, "but instead it seems to have turned into some kind of opportunity for countries to negotiate loopholes and to avoid raising their ambition."

Twenty-two-year-old Hilda Flavia Nakabuye of Uganda also had a powerful message. When she was ten years old, terrible storms hammered the land, ruining her family's crops. Subsequent droughts compelled them to leave their land and seek new means of support. "I came here to represent millions of African young people who are

CLIMATE HERO JAMES HANSEN: SOUNDING THE ALARM

Long before his appearance at the American Geophysical Union in 2007, James Hansen was sounding the alarm on climate change. He became interested in the topic through his studies of Venus, a planet with a surface temperature of 872°F (467°C). In his doctoral dissertation, Hansen speculated that some kind of haze was holding the heat in the atmosphere. A space probe to Venus would later reveal an atmosphere made up of 96 percent carbon dioxide. Hansen's theory was correct. As evidence began to mount of increasing levels of CO_2 and other greenhouse gases on Earth, Hansen abandoned his studies of Venus. He thought it was more important to focus on what was happening on Earth.

In June 1988, Hansen testified before a Senate subcommittee. On a blisteringly hot day, he declared that he was 99 percent certain that an increase of carbon dioxide and other gases in the atmosphere was causing warmer temperatures. "It's time to stop waffling so much and say that the evidence is pretty strong that the greenhouse effect is here," he told reporters afterward. Although Hansen was not the first person to warn about climate change, his testimony marked the beginning of an increased public awareness and concern.

After his historic message to Congress, Hansen continued to warn about climate change. He participated in demonstrations against the use of fossil fuels. In 2013 he was arrested in front of the White House for protesting against the construction of a pipeline that would carry an especially dark, heavy oil. "We have reached a fork in the road," Hansen said, "and the politicians have to understand we either go down this road of exploiting every fossil fuel we have—tar sands, tar shale, offshore drilling in the Arctic—but the science tells us we can't do that without creating a situation where our children will have no control, which is the climate system."

bearing the brunt of the Climate Crisis," she said. "I am the voice of dying children, displaced women, and people suffering at the hands of the climate crisis created by rich countries."

After a session in which both Nakabuye and Thunberg spoke, a group of youth activists marched onto the stage, repeating, "What do we want? Climate justice. When do we want it? Now!" Pounding their message home, they continued. "We are unstoppable," they yelled. "Another world is possible." They hoped that COP26 in Glasgow, Scotland, would bring a more just world closer to reality.

CHAPTER FOUR

ACHIEVING STABILIZED EARTH

On January 17, 2020, Rhode Island governor Gina Raimondo took a bold stance. She signed an executive order to end the state's dependence on fossil fuels within a decade. The mandate specifies that all electricity be powered by renewable energy by 2030. This would make Rhode Island the first state in the Union to achieve that milestone, although California, Hawaii, Maine, New Mexico, New York, Virginia, and Washington State are also working to be free of fossil fuel energy. "As governor of a coastal state and mom to two teenagers, I'm fully committed to protecting the beauty of our state and our way of life for future generations," Raimondo said.

At the time of Raimondo's order, almost all of Rhode Island's electricity came from natural gas. But Nicholas Ucci, acting commissioner of the state's Office of Energy Resources, believes the governor has set a realistic target. "This is an opportune time," he told the *Providence Journal*. "We know how to do this. We've been doing this."

RENEWABLE ENERGY

Although fossil fuels still provide most of the energy consumed in the United States, renewable energy has the potential to take the lead. Often called "clean" energy, renewables depend on natural resources that cannot be depleted such as sunlight, wind, and running water. The National Renewable Energy Laboratory reports that in one hour Earth receives more energy from the sun than the amount of energy used by everyone on the planet in an entire year. From solar rooftop panels that power a single home to giant solar farms that supply power to thousands of homes, solar power is growing. So are other forms of renewable energy. Wind farms with turbines rising many stories into the air also supply power to homes and businesses all over the world. Hydroelectric power (derived from fast-flowing water), geothermal energy (derived from the soaring temperatures inside Earth), and biomass energy (derived from the burning of organic materials such as plants, wood, and dead animals) also make significant contributions to the world's energy supply. According to the International Renewable Energy Agency (IRENA), renewable energy grew to comprise one-third of the worldwide power industry in 2019.

But renewable energy is not perfect. Fossil fuels are used to construct solar panels and wind turbines. They are needed to build dams and to create other technology on which renewable energy depends. So their very construction causes carbon emissions. Consumers need to be aware of the facts and not waste energy just because their homes or businesses are powered by renewables.

Eric Orts is the director of the Initiative for Global Environmental Leadership (IGEL) at the University of Pennsylvania's Wharton School of Business. He stresses that the use of renewable energy should not make its consumers overconfident. "Even with wind and solar, it's not simply zero emission," he said in 2015. "There are manufacturing costs, mining and maintenance issues. It should be said that the movement toward renewables has to be coupled with energy-efficiency efforts. The easiest way to reduce our large-scale carbon footprint is to become a lot more efficient." He believes that businesses can find many ways to reduce their energy consumption.

As the global demand for power grows, however, nonrenewable plants are increasing too. Ken Cook is president of the Environmental

Solar energy capture was discovered in 1839 by a physicist named Alexandre Edmond Becquerel. The first solar array was assembled in 1883 by inventor Charles Fritts. The US started to push for further use of solar power in 1974 after an embargo on oil caused an energy crisis. In 2018 solar power accounted for about 1.5 percent of total overall energy generated in America.

Working Group, a nonprofit research and advocacy organization that studies issues pertaining to agriculture and to ecological dangers. Despite lobbying from the fossil fuel industry and the efforts of some legislators to promote fossil fuels, Cook remains cautiously optimistic. "If we make the right choices, we can create millions of green collar jobs and reverse the climate crisis before it's too late," he said in 2019.

NUCLEAR POWER

Because they are inconsistent in their production, solar and wind power cannot produce all the power the world requires. Solar panels cannot generate power at night or during dark days. Wind farms can only work when strong streams of air are blowing. So wind and solar power should always be supplemented by backup sources of energy. Some climate scientists would like to promote nuclear power as a source of clean, reliable electricity. But they face a great deal of opposition—not only from fossil fuel companies that do not want the competition but also from environmentalists who question the safety of nuclear power. Critics cite the difficulties of safely disposing of nuclear waste and the risk of accidents like the meltdown at Japan's Fukushima Daiichi plant in 2011. Triggered by an earthquake followed by a tsunami, the disaster leaked radiation into the countryside, causing an evacuation of over four hundred thousand people and exposing thirty-two million individuals to serious health risks.

Advocates of nuclear power argue that safer, more efficient nuclear reactors with emergency backup systems are essential to the planet's well-being. Properly run, they believe the chances of a major catastrophe are extremely remote. In 2013 four prominent scientists, including James Hansen, addressed an open letter to environmental activists and world leaders who opposed nuclear power. "While there will be no single technological silver bullet," they wrote, "the time has come for those who take the threat of global warming seriously

The Fukushima Daiichi nuclear power plant has not run since being damaged from the 2011 earthquake and tsunami. While only three of the six reactors experienced a meltdown, the remaining reactors simply store the fuel and contaminated water from the disaster in 2011. Leaked radiation into the surrounding area has left the town of Okuma uninhabitable, and many former residents do not plan to return.

to embrace the development and deployment of safer nuclear power systems as one among several technologies that will be essential to any credible effort to develop an energy system that does not rely on using the atmosphere as a waste dump."

As of 2019, however, two-thirds of the nuclear plants in the United States were threatened with closure. Were these to be replaced by natural gas, the resulting CO_2 emissions would equal about forty-seven million new cars on the road.

NATURAL CARBON SINKS: FOREST AND OCEANS

Phasing out fossil fuels will not reduce the overabundance of carbon dioxide already in the atmosphere. But there are ways to remove some of the excess. Carbon sinks are plants, oceans, or soils that absorb CO_2 from the air and store it. Finding ways to enhance carbon sinks, or increase their capacity to hold carbon, is crucial if temperature rises are to be kept within tolerable limits.

It's estimated that oceans have the potential to hold half the carbon released into the atmosphere by industry and transportation. Corals, fish, algae, certain bacteria, and microscopic organisms known as plankton add considerably to this storage capacity. But ocean acidification is a critical problem. Forests have tremendous potential too. Officials at the IPCC believe that increasing the world's forests by 59 million acres (24 million ha) every year until 2030 would enable them to hold one-quarter of the carbon that must be eliminated from the atmosphere.

SOIL AS A CARBON SINK

More carbon exists in the first 6.6 feet (2 m) of soil on Earth than in the entire atmosphere. Under proper conditions, still more carbon could be stored. But clearing land for farming or overplowing fields causes a loss of topsoil and releases that carbon into the air. Some modern farming techniques and the widespread reliance on chemical fertilizers also hinder the land's capacity to hold carbon.

Carbon farming attempts to remedy this by creating conditions that maximize carbon retention in the soil. Researchers and farmers try to do this in many ways. One is to plant seeds without previously tilling or overturning the earth. This lessens any disturbance of the soil and permits root systems and remains of previous crops to create soil organic matter (SOM) that retains carbon and moisture. Diverse crop rotation is another way farmers can promote an increase of SOM.

Deep-rooted plants such as clovers, alfalfa, and grasses are especially good at furthering SOM production and also provide food for grazing animals. Farmers can further encourage SOM formation by adding compost, wood chips, or animal manure to the soil.

The addition of a substance known as biochar also shows promise as a way to store carbon and, in some cases, to increase ground fertility. Biochar, a high-quality form of charcoal, is formed when materials

CLIMATE HERO JOANNE CHORY AND THE QUEST FOR THE PERFECT PLANT

Nobody knows the importance of plants in fighting climate change better than Joanne Chory. "We have to find a way to take CO_2 out of the atmosphere and I think plants are the only way to do that affordably," Chory said in 2019. A world-renowned botanist, Chory is working to develop plants with an increased capacity to store carbon in their roots. She heads the Harnessing Plants Initiative at the Salk Institute for Biological Studies in San Diego. Through genetic manipulation, Chory and her colleagues hope to evolve plants with stronger systems that contain greater amounts of suberin, a corklike substance that holds carbon. According to Chory, the plants with enhanced root systems will also decrease erosion, improve soils, and lead to bigger crop yields. When the plants die, their deep roots will continue to hold considerable amounts of carbon for long periods. Eventually, Chory and her team hope to boost the carbon-holding capacity of the most widely grown crops such as corn, wheat, cotton, rice, and rapeseed, and field covers that are not used for food. If farmers across the world grew enhanced plants, Chory's team calculates that atmospheric CO_2 levels could fall by as much as 46 percent each year. "It's a philosophic issue, too," Chory has said of her work. "If I take pain now [make sacrifices], maybe my great-grandchildren might see a benefit. People choose no pain now, and that's why we've done nothing about climate change."

such as plant wastes, wood scraps, and sewage sludge are heated at high temperatures with little or no oxygen present. Biochar locks in the carbon and stores it in the ground where it can remain sequestered for centuries. Some researchers argue that biochar could retain billions of tons of carbon dioxide each year.

WETLANDS

Wetlands, such as marshes and swamps, contain dense plant life, algae, and soils that make them important carbon sinks. Although they only cover about 3 percent of Earth's surface, they are estimated to hold between 20 and 30 percent of all carbon that is stored in soil. Environmentalists stress the importance of preserving wetlands, rehabilitating wetlands that have been harmed, and creating new wetlands to replace those that have been destroyed

In Uganda, Eco-Fuel Africa workers press agricultural waste into a machine to produce a powder, which may be compressed into a biofuel that burns longer than charcoal, or used as a fertilizer. The fuel is clean, inexpensive, and prevents further deforestation for firewood.

for commercial and real estate development. Acknowledging the huge amount of carbon stored in soils, Siobhan Fennessy, coauthor of a 2016 study, says that wetlands contain "a hugely disproportionate amount of that carbon." Fennessy and her colleague Amanda Nahlik have determined that the amount of carbon stored in wetlands in the United States roughly equals four years of fossil fuel emissions by the nation.

ON THE GO

According to the American Lung Association, over 133.9 million Americans live in areas where pollution rises to unhealthy levels. Anyone who has driven through a major metropolitan area during rush hour knows that car exhausts contribute significantly to air pollution. For many years, environmentalists have called for carpooling and a greater use of mass transit systems as one way to reduce the number of cars on the road.

More efficient engines that get higher gas mileage per gallon can also help lessen carbon emissions. Battery-powered hybrid cars use both gas and electricity and can go up to 70 miles (113 km) on 1 gallon (3.8 L) of gas. Cars that run entirely on electricity provide even greater benefits in gas mileage and emissions reductions. These vehicles are powered by the electric grid that services consumers, by small home renewable energy systems, or both. How well they benefit the environment depends on the source of their power. If the electricity used to power them comes from fossil fuels, they are not as environmentally friendly as they should be.

BIOFUELS: PROS AND CONS

Gasoline and electricity aren't the only ways to power a car. Biofuels also offer promise for future modes of transportation. Made from organic matter such as corn, sugar beets, and potatoes or from vegetable oils and fats, biofuels are designed to supplement or replace gasoline or diesel in cars. Like fossil fuels, biofuels, such as ethanol, discharge a great deal of carbon as they burn. But the new crops continually planted to keep up the production of biofuels absorb much of this carbon. How these crops are handled determines how effective biofuels actually are. If a great deal of fossil fuel is used in fertilizing, harvesting, and processing the crops and then transporting the final product, much of the benefit is lost.

In 2007 the US Congress passed the Energy Independence

HYDROGEN-POWERED VEHICLES

A new and relatively unknown type of electric car, the hydrogen-powered vehicle, may soon be making news. Instead of using an onboard battery or an electrical outlet to recharge, hydrogen vehicles depend on fuel cells that mix hydrogen with oxygen to generate electricity. The only emissions produced are water and water vapor. No fumes or exhaust are released into the atmosphere. But since these cars must be refueled with hydrogen, the shortage of hydrogen service stations limits their use. Another drawback is the large amount of energy needed to separate hydrogen from other elements and compress it. Although most commercial hydrogen is generated through the use of fossil fuels, it can also come from solar and wind power as well as other renewable sources. Mitch Ewan of the University of Hawaii has called hydrogen "the perfect fuel of the future."

The University of California, Irvine, uses eco-friendly buses that run on hydrogen fuel cells.

and Security Act requiring that biofuel production increase from 4.7 billion gallons (18 billion L) in that year to 36 billion gallons (136 billion L) by 2022. Based on the bill's mandate, more than 2.8 million additional acres (1.1 million ha) nationwide were given over to cropland for biofuels between 2008 and 2016. But this meant the loss of many wetlands, prairies, and forests. Carbon held in the trees, roots, plants, and soils of these terrains was released into the air. Many species of wildlife, including butterflies, bees, and other animals that pollinate plants lost their habitats. Growing crops for biofuels also took over lands that had been used for food crops. So the cost of food rose. Newer or more advanced biofuels, made from nonfood plant parts or animal waste products, reduce the competition for land use. The benefits and disadvantages of biofuels continue to be debated.

AVIATION

Flying had become routine for meteorologist Eric Holthaus. As a reporter covering weather events and climate change, he traveled frequently to Africa and the Caribbean. In 2012 he logged about 75,000 miles (120,700 km). But the IPCC Report of 2013, which stressed the need for immediate reductions in greenhouse gases, caused him to reevaluate. Speaking to his wife from the airport before yet another flight, Holthaus realized the importance of individual commitment to saving the environment. "And that's why," he wrote in 2013, "my wife and I suddenly knew we could never fly again." Later, when he crunched the numbers, he was stunned to find that half of his household's greenhouse emissions for the previous year came from air travel—a whopping total of 37 tons (34 t) of CO_2.

Airline flights released about 860 million tons (780 million t) of carbon dioxide into the atmosphere in 2017. As the public demand for air travel continues to grow, airlines are adding more flights to their schedules. In 2018, 4.3 billion passengers worldwide traveled by air, 38 million more than the previous year. Yet the aviation industry has pledged that by 2050, its emissions will be half of what they were in 2005.

To meet their commitment, airlines will have to make major changes. Although some people have expressed interest in electric

RENEWABLE ENERGY AT A GLANCE

SOLAR POWER–Catches the sun's light in solar panels composed of photoelectric cells that convert the light into electricity.

WIND POWER–Uses the strength of the wind to rotate the blades of wind turbines. An electrical generator transforms this movement into electricity.

HYDROELECTRIC ENERGY–Uses the force of rapidly moving water released from a dam to spin the blades of a turbine, thereby triggering a generator to produce electricity.

GEOTHERMAL ENERGY–Uses steam from basins of hot water miles below Earth's surface to spin the blades of a turbine, which activates a generator to produce electricity.

BIOMASS ENERGY–The burning of organic matter hot gas is passed through a steam engine or a steam turbine to generate electricity.

planes or planes powered by hydrogen, such aircraft probably won't be implemented for at least several decades. Sustainable aviation fuel, an advanced type of biofuel, offers another possible pathway to lower airplane emissions. Between 2008 and 2019, biofuels (blended with regular jet fuels) have powered more than 150,000 flights. But biofuels have made almost no dent in airline emissions. By 2018 annual production of biofuels made up less than 0.1 percent of aviation fuel being used. Research continues on ways to make sustainable aviation fuel more practical and available.

Meanwhile, a United Nations plan, known as the Carbon Offsetting and Reduction Scheme for International Aviation (CORSIA) would allow airlines to buy credits that lessen emissions in other sectors. Although airline CO_2 emissions do not actually diminish

MINUSES OF RENEWABLE ENERGY

- Large amounts of fossil fuel are required to create facilities and distribution networks.
- The amount of power produced is affected by weather. Lack of sunshine, wind, or rain lessens the amount of power generated.
- This inconsistent output of power means that energy must be stored in batteries or through other means for future use. The technology exists and is becoming more reasonable in price but can still be expensive.
- Power stations for renewable energy require more physical space than power stations that run on fossil fuels.
- Renewable energy is difficult to generate in the same quantities that fossil fuels provide.

PLUSES OF RENEWABLE ENERGY

- Sources of renewable energy are abundant and cannot be depleted.
- No carbon dioxide, other greenhouse gases, or pollutants are emitted.
- Absence of atmospheric contaminants benefits those with cardiac and respiratory problems by not polluting the air.
- Nations can become energy independent instead of relying on countries with large amounts of fossil fuels.
- In the long run, renewable energy stations are less expensive to operate and maintain than those dependent on fossil fuels.

under the plan, they are canceled out by the reductions that take place elsewhere. Carbon credits may come from a variety of projects, including wind power, methane capture, forest planting, and other activities that reduce greenhouse emissions. But CORSIA, which has been accepted by 192 countries, does not eliminate the airlines' responsibility to pursue new technologies and sustainable fuels.

NATURE DOESN'T CARE
HOW HARD WE TRIED

Reducing emissions through renewable energy sources and enhancing carbon sinks is vitally important. But what if these efforts aren't enough to stop climate change? Jeffrey D. Sachs is the director of the Earth Institute at Columbia University. "Nature doesn't care how hard we tried," he said in 2010. "Nature cares how high the parts per million levels rise. [The atmospheric level of CO_2] is running away." For this reason, many climate scientists, including the authors of the "Trajectories" paper believe we must turn to technology—some form of geoengineering, not only to reduce current emissions but also to remove CO_2 that human activities have already released into the air.

CHAPTER FIVE

GEOENGINEERING

The name Pleistocene Park may call to mind the blockbuster book and sci-fi film *Jurassic Park*. This real-life geoengineering project aims to re-create the Siberian landscape of ten thousand years ago and to help slow climate change. Russian scientist Sergey Zimov conceived of the vast experiment after he realized, in the 1990s, that winters in Siberia weren't as cold as they used to be.

This was especially alarming because he calculated that the permafrost in and around the Arctic Circle could contain as much as 1 trillion tons (0.9 trillion t) of carbon, or twice as much as previous estimates. If the permafrost began to melt—and Zimov believed this was close to happening—the results would be catastrophic. "This [the far Northern Hemisphere] is the most dangerous territory in the world in terms of climate change," he has asserted.

Zimov believes the danger can be averted or at least mitigated by changing the ecology of the area. During the Pleistocene, he reasons, much of what has become Siberia, northern Asia, and Canada was covered with grassy pastures. Large herbivores (plant-eating animals) such as mammoths, reindeer, moose, and musk oxen inhabited the area. When humans moved in, these animals were hunted to extinction. Forests and shrubs replaced the grasslands. Although trees and shrubs hold carbon, they are darker and absorb more heat than grass. But if grazing animals were reintroduced in the area, several important benefits would result. First, the hooves of the heavy animals would flatten the snow. This compressed snow would keep permafrost colder than less densely packed snow would. As another plus, herbivores would eat the dark shrubs. Moving through the forests, the bulky animals would help topple trees, giving the grasslands a chance to return. These grasslands would store vast amounts of carbon in their roots. Finally, grassy pastures are lighter in color than forests and so reflect more heat rather than absorb it.

Millions of animals would be needed to transform the land. As of 2018, however, only ninety animals had been transplanted to Pleistocene Park, which Sergey Zimov's son Nikita Zimov helps manage. These include grazers native to the area in the Pleistocene era as well as others such as yaks and sheep that never lived there. What the elder Zimov would like most is a herd of woolly mammoths. Unfortunately, this enormous relative of the elephant went extinct more than thirty-six hundred years ago. Plans are underway, however, to create a hybrid animal with DNA from a mammoth that was buried

These semi-wild Yakutian horses are some of the first animals that were introduced to Pleistocene Park. The horses are native to Siberia and have adapted long coats to survive the frigid temperatures. They are gathered near the caretaker's cabin on the 40,000-acre (16,187 ha) park.

in the ice forty-two thousand years ago, a project that will take many years to complete with no guarantee of success.

To ensure the best results in his fight against climate change, Zimov would like to found as many as ten parks, including ones in Canada and Alaska. As trees fall and are washed away and grasses spread, the parks would expand outward to form a single vast ecological region.

ARTIFICIAL TREES—MIMICKING PHOTOSYNTHESIS

Pleistocene Park is just one of many geoengineering proposals to lessen or reverse climate change. Still considered controversial by many people, geoengineering projects fall into one of two categories: carbon capture, to suck CO_2 and other greenhouse gases from the air, and solar geoengineering, to control atmospheric temperature by deflecting sunlight back into space. Pleistocene Park would attempt to restore a vast carbon sink through carbon capture. But a number of other carbon capture projects loom on the horizon. One project mimics photosynthesis.

Artificial or mechanical "trees" may not look like their biological counterparts, but they use CO_2 and water and emit oxygen, just as real plants do. Invented by Klaus Lackner of Arizona State University, one promising variety consists of metal frames with hundreds of resin-filled strips. The wind blows through the "tree," allowing the strips to capture carbon from the air and convert it to bicarbonate, the same substance in baking soda. When the strips are filled to capacity, they are pulled into a container filled with water. This prompts chemical reactions that will liberate the concentrated CO_2 gas as the water is drained away. The strips can then be returned to their original position to capture more carbon. The recaptured CO_2 can be stored away (perhaps injected into the ground), used to produce synthetic fuels, or sold for industrial purposes.

The process is far from perfect. Mechanical trees only absorb carbon when the wind is blowing through them. They only work in dry climates because humidity lets the CO_2 escape back into the atmosphere. But advocates of mechanical trees point out that they are "thousands of times more efficient" than natural trees. A two-year test of the technology, conducted by Silicon Kingdom Holdings, a start-up based in Dublin, with Arizona State University, proved very successful. In 2019 the company planned a larger project with twelve hundred mechanical trees. The arrangement would absorb 40,235 tons (36,500 t) of carbon each year, the same amount eight thousand cars would be expected to emit. It's estimated that a large-scale mechanical tree farm could capture 3.8 million tons (3.4 million t) of CO_2 each year.

Klaus Lackner stands beside a prototype of his "mechanical tree." Other scientists have come up with similar ideas, but Lackner's tree is passive, which means it does not suck air in but waits for wind to blow. This makes the machine less costly as it does not expend as much energy to convert CO_2 to oxygen.

CLIMATE HERO WALLACE BROECKER: THE CLIMATE SYSTEM IS AN ANGRY BEAST

When Wallace Broecker (1931–2019) coined the phrase "global warming" in a scientific paper he published in 1975, he had no idea how widespread the term would become. He disliked the honorary titles "grandfather of climate science" and "father of global warming" that were often bestowed on him. But Broecker was one of the first scientists to call attention to the relationship between CO_2 emissions and a possible rise in global temperatures. He was especially interested in how ocean currents and CO_2 absorption affected weather patterns. Often he called the climate system "an angry beast [that] we are poking with sticks."

Broecker wrote over five hundred scientific papers and seventeen books. He received many awards and millions of dollars of prize money that he used for his research. In 1996 President Bill Clinton presented him with the National Medal of Science.

Worried about the steady rise of CO_2 emissions and pessimistic that they would be substantially reduced, Broecker became interested in technological ways to mitigate climate change. One of his last projects was to help organize a symposium on the topic at Arizona State University. Broecker was too ill to attend the conference. Seated in a wheelchair, he spoke with participants through a live broadcast. "If we are going to prevent the planet from warming up another couple of degrees, we are going to have to go to geoengineering," he declared. Failure to do so, he predicted, could lead to "many more surprises in the greenhouse," (by which he meant Earth). Seven days later, Broecker died at the age of eighty-seven. His final message, coming so close to his passing, revitalized the debate on the pros and cons of geoengineering.

POTENTIAL AND RISKS OF CARBON REMOVAL

In exploring ways to reduce the global temperature rise, the IPCC has created over 1,000 computer simulations. Only 116 kept temperatures within acceptable limits. Of these, 101 depended on carbon removal from the atmosphere.

A variety of different ways to pull carbon out of the air are being researched as companies seek ways to lower costs and use recaptured carbon. Climeworks, based in Switzerland, markets carbon to fertilizer and fuel manufacturers. Climeworks plans to sell CO_2 to the beverage industry for carbonated drinks. Carbon Engineering, founded by physicist David Keith of Harvard University and based in Canada, combines CO_2 with hydrogen to produce a clean liquid fuel. Although CO_2 is emitted when the fuel is burned, it had been pulled from the air. No new carbon is added to the atmosphere, making the fuel carbon neutral.

Despite the promise of carbon removal, however, many people, including Keith, call for caution. Huge amounts of technology would have to be installed to significantly affect greenhouse levels. The widespread usage could give people a false sense of security and lessen their commitment to reducing their personal CO_2 emissions. "It's a huge concern," Tzeporah Berman of the environmental group Stand.earth said in 2019. "These technologies provide a false hope that we can continue to depend on fossil fuels and produce and burn them, and technology will fix it. We are way past that point." Much research remains, and there is no guarantee that carbon removal, no matter how widespread, can maintain the conditions that support human life on Earth.

SOLAR GEOENGINEERING: VOLCANOES

Many people fear that reduced emissions and carbon capture will not be enough to halt climate change. What if it were possible to deflect a portion of the sun's heat back into space before it reached Earth? One way that solar geoengineering attempts to do this is by mimicking volcanic eruptions. When a volcano erupts, it spews sulfur dioxide gas into the air. Over the next several weeks and months, the gas is converted to droplets or aerosols that spread across the globe high in the upper levels of the atmosphere. They remain for about two years, deflecting sunlight from Earth and cooling temperatures in the lower atmosphere. The eruption of Mount Pinatubo in the Philippines in 1991 ejected about 20 million tons (18 million t) of sulfur dioxide and lowered global temperatures by about 1.1°F (0.6°C) for fifteen months. Stratospheric aerosol injection (SAI) would attempt to produce a similar effect by discharging tiny particles into the upper atmosphere.

According to a study published in 2018, a new type of plane that flies higher than current aircraft would be required to undertake SAI missions. Once developed, SAI could begin with eight planes flying four thousand missions a year. Within fifteen years, the fleet would be expected to grow to almost one hundred planes flying over

REWINDING THE EMISSIONS CLOCK

What if we could undo some of the greenhouse emissions of the last thirty years?

Scientists at RMIT University in Melbourne, Australia, have developed a way to convert gaseous CO_2 from the burning of fossil fuels back into coal. The CO_2 is dissolved in an electrolyte liquid, a liquid containing charged particles. After a small quantity of liquid metal is added, an electrical current is passed through the solution. The carbon dioxide is converted into particles of solid carbon that fall to the bottom of the container. An international research team from Australia, the United States, China, and Germany believe the technique could lead to a large-scale and inexpensive way to lessen the amount of CO_2 in the atmosphere. "While we can't literally turn back time," said RMIT researcher Torben Daeneke, "turning carbon dioxide back into coal and burying it back in the ground is a bit like rewinding the emissions clock."

sixty thousand missions annually. But although SAI could help cool temperatures, it does nothing to reduce the growing level of greenhouse gases in the atmosphere. It does not address the urgent problem of ocean acidification. And if the aerosol spraying flights were stopped, temperatures would soar within a few years.

Despite its possible benefits, a great deal of uncertainty surrounds SAI. No one can predict how aerosol spraying might affect global weather patterns, and climate experts agree on the need for more research.

MORE WAYS TO REFLECT THE SUN'S HEAT

Many other ideas have been put forth to counter climate change. A technique called marine cloud brightening would spray salt water into clouds over the ocean. This would make the clouds larger and lighter, able to reflect more sunlight and heat away from Earth. Large mirrors, or arrangements of mirrors, launched into space would also bounce sunlight back into space.

Even something as simple as bubbles can make a difference. One proposal would employ ships to stir up millions of tiny bubbles on the top of the ocean. Studies from the University College London indicate that ocean foam could reflect ten times as much sunlight as the ocean itself does. Another idea—brightening the landscape by painting buildings white—could potentially alleviate health problems in cities during heat waves but would not have an impact on global temperatures.

GIVE ME HALF A TANKER OF IRON

In 1988 oceanographer John Martin stood up during a seminar at the Woods Hole Oceanographic Institution in Massachusetts and declared, "Give me half a tanker of iron, and I will give you an ice age." Although he spoke somewhat jokingly, his words stimulated research into the possibility of iron fertilization. This entails covering large areas of the ocean's surface with iron, probably as iron sulfate crystals. The iron increases the growth of phytoplankton, tiny ocean plants that absorb

This aerial view of the ocean was captured by a NASA satellite equipped with an imaging system to take true-color images of Earth's oceans. The swirls of green, teal, and turquoise in the water are phytoplankton in bloom. This bloom covers about 80 percent of the ocean off Iceland's coast. Phytoplankton is an important food source for many marine creatures including shrimp, snails, jellyfish, and whales.

CO_2 and release oxygen. Proponents of this strategy reason that large amounts of iron deposited in the ocean could potentially lower the level of atmospheric CO_2, though computer models do not bear this out.

Just like other forms of geoengineering, iron fertilization carries significant risks. When the masses of phytoplankton nourished by iron die, their decaying bodies attract bacteria. Huge numbers of bacteria can use up all the oxygen in an area, causing fish to die off. Dead zones, or large areas void of oxygen and life, would result.

"POSSIBLE, BUT UNPROVEN"

No form of geoengineering can be considered a quick fix, and the risks, both scientific and political, are significant. "More research on the topic could just as easily reveal reasons not to do it as reasons to do it," Jane Flegal, an expert on geoengineering, said in 2017. For example, aerosols injected into the stratosphere over the Northern Hemisphere might cool that part of the globe by a small amount. The injections could possibly lessen hurricanes in the North Atlantic, but they might cause severe drought in sub-Saharan Africa. If SAI were used in the Southern Hemisphere, the benefits and disasters would be reversed. While sub-Saharan Africa experienced greater rainfall, the number of tropical cyclones reaching the eastern United States would also go up. Many people worry that nations will not be able to agree on how to use geoengineering—or whether to use it at all. In the absence of an international agreement, nothing could stop one country from acting unilaterally in what seems to be its own best interest. As with carbon removal techniques, solar geoengineering might lull people into the false belief that the problem of climate change has been solved. Politicians might lessen their commitment to curbing their country's carbon emissions. They might take funds from desperately needed programs to protect areas at risk for wildfires or hurricanes and channel it into risky geoengineering ventures.

David Keith summarized the general attitude at the Climate Engineering Conference held in Berlin in 2017. "In my view, solar geoengineering is—at best—a supplement to emissions cuts, not a substitute for them. It is possible that a combination of emissions cuts, carbon removal and solar geoengineering could provide a significantly safer climate than emissions cuts alone or emissions cuts and carbon removal combined. Possible, but unproven."

CHAPTER SIX

SOCIAL JUSTICE AND CLIMATE CHANGE

Benetick Kabua Maddison was only five when an especially high tide surged into his home in the Marshall Islands. "I was in [water] up to my waist," Maddison, then a college student in the United States, said in 2016, "I remember toys, blankets scattered everywhere. My father grabbed me. It was very frightening. The entire island was flooded."

King tides engulf the Majuro capital city of the Marshall Islands. These higher than normal tides can be caused by specific alignments of the sun, Earth, and moon. However, they are also caused by storms—even hundreds or thousands of miles away. The Marshall Islands, as well as other coastal or island dwellings, are at extreme risk of being completely submerged as sea levels rise and weather conditions become more volatile.

As sea levels rise, the future of the Maddison's homeland becomes progressively more critical. Consisting of more than twelve hundred islands and inlets in the central Pacific Ocean, the Marshall Islands are only 3 to 6.6 feet (1 to 2 m) above sea level. The strip of land on which the capital city of Majuro sits is only 300 feet wide (91 m) but crowded with over twenty-seven thousand residents. Devastating "king tides" routinely submerge the seawalls, filling the streets with debris and raw sewage. Salt water creeps into the soil, stunting the breadfruit trees that islanders cultivate and contaminating drinking water. Powerful tropical storms pound the islands' shores, ravage its fisheries, and damage the coral reefs, or atolls, that comprise much of the environment. And they batter a concrete dome that stores radioactive waste from the testing of nuclear bombs. Between 1946 and 1958, the United States detonated sixty-seven bombs in the Marshall Islands. Storms and floods threaten to crack the dome, leaking its radioactive contents into the ocean.

The nuclear bomb detonation at Bikini Atoll of the Marshall Islands was the first underwater test of an atomic bomb. The area was declared a wasteland after the US dropped twenty-three bombs over the island. The plants and animals were contaminated and deemed inedible. Many of the residents suffered from illnesses brought on by nuclear radiation.

Marshall Islander Lani Kramer believes that the United States has not done nearly enough to compensate her country or to help those who got cancer from the radioactive fallout. She worries that her country may have suffered through the dangers of nuclear testing only to succumb to climate change. "When the next uprising from the sea comes and washes away all the crops and stuff from people's houses, then what?" she said in 2016. "We are going to go under. The water is going to keep coming up and we're going to have nowhere else to go. We're going to have no place."

CLIMATE INJUSTICE

The Marshall Islands and other island countries such as Kiribati, Tuvalu, and the Maldives have contributed almost nothing to the world's greenhouse gas emissions. Yet they suffer far more damaging consequences from climate change than the much wealthier nations that have sent vast amounts of carbon into the atmosphere. According to researchers from Stanford University, climate change furthers the inequality between the richest and poorest nations. Tropical African nations have been especially hard hit, both environmentally and economically. Excessively high temperatures hinder labor productivity, cause cognitive decline, and provoke personal conflicts.

Poor countries are unprepared for weather disasters like Cyclone Idai that swept across Mozambique, Malawi, and Zimbabwe in March 2019, causing more than a thousand deaths and forcing hundreds of thousands from their homes. In the aftermath of tragedy, underdeveloped nations lack the funds to provide adequate relief and to rebuild. Money may have to be diverted from other pressing needs like education and health care to build seawalls and storm water drains or repair damaged roads, bridges, and power facilities. In the case of drought, the funds may be needed to construct irrigation systems. People need more support than the government can give them to recover from severe weather events, rising sea levels, or devastating droughts. "We're not arguing that global warming created inequality," climate scientist Noah Diffenbaugh of Stanford University said in 2019. But "global warming has put a drag on improvement."

Volunteers and residents work together to clean and rebuild after an earthquake and tsunami in December of 2004 devastated the coasts of fourteen countries including India, Indonesia, Thailand, Malaysia, and Sri Lanka. The waves from the tsunami reached 98 feet (30 m), and the disaster is one of the deadliest natural disasters in history. The affected areas were rebuilt, but the landscape was changed forever.

CLIMATE HERO TONY DE BRUM: HIGH AMBITION COALITION

In March 1954, nine-year-old Tony de Brum was fishing with his grandfather in the Marshall Islands when his world changed suddenly. As an elderly man, he recalled the frightening scene, "Everything turned red—the ocean, the fish, the sky, and my grandfather's net." The United States had just tested a nuclear bomb, one thousand times as powerful as those that had devastated Hiroshima and Nagasaki in Japan at the end of World War II (1939–1945). Even 200 miles (322 km) away from the blast, Tony was shaken to his core.

Many years later, as the foreign minister of the Marshall Islands, de Brum would often draw a connection between nuclear testing and climate change. Radioactive fallout from the tests had forced many Marshallese to leave their homes for other islands. De Brum knew that rising sea levels could cause another evacuation, a situation he called "repugnant." To prevent this, de Brum went to the UN Climate Change Conference in 2015 determined to fight for his country and for all island nations. "Displacement of populations and destruction of cultural language and tradition is equivalent in our minds to genocide," he declared before the talks began.

Managing to bridge the gap between rich and poor countries, de Brum organized a group of about one hundred nations into what became known as the high ambition coalition. During the tense negotiations, the group pressed successfully for a goal in which nations would strive to limit global temperature rise to 2.7°F (1.5°C) above preindustrial levels by 2100. De Brum emphasized that a 3.6°F (2°C) rise would be disastrous for low-lying nations like the Marshall Islands. He also lobbied for zero carbon emissions by 2050. Marshall Islands president Hilda Heine praised de Brum as "a real hero, a giant of history, a custodian of our shared future."

NO COUNTRY IS SAFE

All across the world, it is the poor who suffer the most from climate change. The US Defense Department has referred to the consequences of climate change as "threat multipliers that will aggravate stressors abroad such as poverty, environmental degradation, political stability, and social tensions." Even in affluent nations like the United States, financially struggling individuals face disproportionate hardships. For example, when Hurricane Katrina slammed New Orleans in 2005, some people lacked cars to drive to a safer location. Others in poor-quality housing could not afford to ride out the storm in the greater safety of a motel. Because low-income neighborhoods sometimes exist close to industrial areas, residents may be endangered when violent weather causes hazardous materials to leak into the environment. One of the most tragic weather events in recent times occurred in 2017 when Hurricane Maria devastated Puerto Rico. According to a study from George Washington University, 2,975

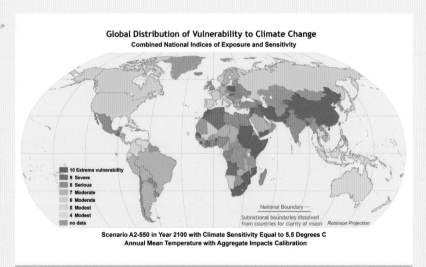

This map of the world shows the countries that are most impacted by climate change according to a study done by Wesleyan University and Columbia University. Parts of Africa, Asia, and Europe are the most vulnerable to the higher temperatures caused by climate change. The US is moderately vulnerable to these changes.

people died. Many of these people survived the actual storm, but roads that were flooded or destroyed kept them from reaching the hospital for urgent medical care. Those with serious health conditions did not have access to lifesaving medicines. Racial minorities are especially likely to suffer financial loss and lack of health care.

WOMEN, CHILDREN, AND THE ELDERLY

Women, children, and the elderly are particularly susceptible to the hardships of climate change. Many rural communities in underdeveloped countries depend on women and children to gather firewood and fetch water. Hotter temperatures and increased droughts make their task more physically challenging. They must go farther to get provisions, and they have less time to focus on other chores. Climate change poses a greater health risk to the young and the old than to the rest of the population. They are more likely to be weakened by soaring temperatures, malnourishment, and waterborne diseases from floods. Although many women are the heads of their households, they often must struggle for opportunities to acquire land, resources, and climate-resistant crops and technology—advantages that are more freely given to men.

A FUNDAMENTAL REORIENTATION OF HUMAN VALUES

Science alone cannot handle all the political, social, legal, and economic ramifications of climate change. For this reason, many people advocate for an intersectional approach to climate change that considers gender, race, social issues, and economics. Will Steffen, Johan Rockström, and the other authors of the "Trajectories" paper believe that solving the climate crisis should also address poverty, inequality, and social injustice. They call for nothing less than "a deep transformation based on a fundamental reorientation of human values, equity, behavior, institutions, economies, and technologies."

In such a worldview, the planet's resources would be carefully conserved and shared equally among all people. Preserving ecological balances would replace maximizing profits as a key human value. This would lead to a situation "in which humanity plays an active planetary stewardship role" to achieve and maintain a "Stabilized Earth." Men and women would be responsible for the well-being of all Earth systems—including the geosphere (land, rocks), hydrosphere (water), atmosphere (air), and biosphere (living things). Instead of exploiting Earth for their own needs, stewards would value Earth for itself and treat it with respect.

The shifts in attitude and behavior, as well as education and institutions that are required to reach this state of stewardship, won't happen overnight. The "Trajectories" authors think that some may take decades. But they see signs that humanity may be reaching some significant "tipping points" toward the right direction. As an example, they cite the expansion of women's horizons through more educational opportunities, access to health care, and higher income levels. Besides giving women a better chance to preserve Earth, these benefits are consistent with a lowering of the birth rate. This is important because fewer people means fewer resources consumed.

NO SILVER BULLETS

The "Trajectories" paper does not tell us how to make all the necessary transformations to avoid a hothouse Earth scenario. That remains an open challenge. Chad Frischmann is the research director and vice president of Project Drawdown, an organization that studies ways to lower, or draw down, levels of atmospheric CO_2. In his 2018 TED (Technology, Entertainment, Design) talk "100 Solutions to Reverse Climate Warming," he reiterated that there are "no silver bullets" to reach that goal, no easy fixes. He believes that the many solutions offered by Project Drawdown all have important roles in fighting climate change. "But here's the great thing," he said at his TED talk.

INDIGENOUS PEOPLES: A RELATIONSHIP WITH THE LAND

The authors of "Trajectories of the Earth System in the Anthropocene" call on humanity to assume a stewardship role toward the environment. But for indigenous peoples across the globe, caring for Earth and all living creatures has long been a way of life. Jon Waterhouse, an Indigenous Peoples Scholar at Oregon Health and Science University, believes that the world has a great deal to learn from them. "As a global community, we have lost our way; we forgot what it means to have a relationship with the land. . . . Indigenous peoples have mastered the art of living on the Earth without destroying it."

The Sápara, or Záparo, and other indigenous peoples of the Amazon rain forest provide an outstanding example. By respecting and nurturing the land, they have managed to preserve healthy ecosystems with diverse species of plants and animals that help lessen the effects of climate change. But the Sápara culture faces fierce resistance to their traditions and their sustainable management. "The government of Ecuador continues to view [indigenous] peoples as an obstacle to economic growth," Kevin Koenig, climate and energy director of the environmental group Amazon Watch, said in 2018. "It is pushing for oil development in the region by auctioning off blocks of the Sápara's Naku (sacred rain forest). . . ." But Koenig believes that protecting the Naku is the most important thing the Sápara could do to fight climate change and preserve plant and animal species.

All over the world as developers have encroached on their territories—clearing forests, damming rivers to generate electricity, desecrating Earth in pursuit of oil and natural gas—native populations have fought to save the environment.

In Canada, supporters of the Wet'suwet'en First Nation marched in protest at the construction of a pipeline through Wet'suwet'en ancestral land. These rallies have occurred throughout Canada in 2019 and 2020.

But their efforts have met with a great deal of resistance and even violence. When indigenous people protest the disruption of the ecology of their lands without permission, they often face harassment, false accusations, and even prison. According to the environmental and human rights group Global Witness, in 2017 at least 207 activists were murdered for trying to save forests and rivers from exploitation by big industry. Almost half of the victims were indigenous people fighting for their homelands. In response to what has been called a "global crisis," the United Nations has launched a global campaign to fight the "criminalization" of indigenous peoples.

"We would want to implement these solutions whether or not global warming was even a problem, because they have cascading benefits to human and planetary well-being." For example, renewable electricity is good for the environment and can also provide energy to people in developing countries who might not otherwise have power. Plant-based diets and conservation of food resources help lower CO_2 emissions, and it also helps assure that there will be enough for the growing world population. Family planning and educational opportunities for women help individuals as well as the environment. "This is about human rights, about gender equality," Frischmann said. "This is about economic improvement and the freedom of choice. It's about justice."

SUSTAINABLE DEVELOPMENT GOALS

The United Nations acknowledged the relationship between climate change and human rights issues in September 2015 when it adopted seventeen Sustainable Development Goals. Taking a holistic approach to urgent global crises, the goals are meant to assure that all people experience economic, social, and physical well-being. The goals cover the following areas and challenge governments and businesses to create a world with the following characteristics:

1. NO POVERTY
2. ZERO HUNGER
3. GOOD HEALTH AND WELL-BEING
4. QUALITY EDUCATION
5. GENDER EQUALITY
6. CLEAN WATER AND SANITATION
7. AFFORDABLE AND CLEAN ENERGY
8. DECENT WORK AND ECONOMIC GROWTH
9. INDUSTRY, INNOVATION, AND INFRASTRUCTURE
10. REDUCED INEQUALITY
11. SUSTAINABLE CITIES AND COMMUNITIES

12. **RESPONSIBLE CONSUMPTION AND PRODUCTION**
13. **CLIMATE ACTION**
14. **LIFE BELOW WATER**
15. **LIFE ON LAND**
16. **PEACE, JUSTICE, AND STRONG INSTITUTIONS**
17. **PARTNERSHIPS TO ACHIEVE THE GOAL**

In his book, *Big World, Small Planet*, Johan Rockström hailed the Sustainable Development Goals as "the first time, world leaders discussed that global sustainability is a prerequisite for poverty alleviation (reduction) and that rising global environmental risks may undermine future progress in development." So the seventeen goals cannot be separated from one another. The achievement of any one depends on progress in the others. Seen through an intersectional lens, climate change impacts many aspects of society. Then the key to fighting climate change lies in rigorously pursuing justice, equality, and prosperity for all people. "The window of success is still open," Rockström reminded people in a 2018 TED talk. "The earth system is still resilient. . . . But we need radically different thinking."

CHAPTER SEVEN

ADAPTATION: PREPARING FOR AN UNCERTAIN FUTURE

The enormous triple-decker cube in Rotterdam's harbor is what some people think the future will look like. The world's first floating dairy farm, it boasts a top level of greenhouses, a middle level for cows milked by robots, and a lower level of machines to process milk and yogurt. Powered by solar energy, the farm is capable of functioning even when storms and rising sea levels flood the land. This is especially important because nine-tenths of Rotterdam lies below sea level. Factor in climate change, and the city is in serious jeopardy. Already rising oceans have taken over much of the farmland in the Netherlands.

Dutch engineer Peter van Wingerden didn't get the idea for the floating farm in his homeland, however. He happened to be in New York City when Hurricane Sandy struck in 2012. Streets flooded, food distribution stalled, and stores ran out of fresh fruits and vegetables. "Seeing the devastation caused by Hurricane Sandy I was struck by the need for food to be produced as near as possible to consumers," van Wingerden said in 2018. His "hurricane resistant" farm would ensure Rotterdam a steady supply of dairy goods in even the worst scenario.

Also home to a three-domed floating pavilion that can accommodate up to five hundred guests, Rotterdam has captured world attention for its striking examples of climate adaptation. Its floating park, composed of recycled plastic waste, protects the environment and boosts climate resilience. Rotterdam's mobile storm surge barrier guards the channel between the city and the North Sea. It is controlled by a supercomputer that automatically shuts the enormous gate when rising waters threaten to flood the city. "We [the Dutch] were already busy with the climate change before it was worldwide," Peter Persoon, a former engineer and tour guide at the barrier, said in 2016. "What we are busy with is the future. What are the circumstances in 2100? That's why we are preparing our country."

In 2019 Peter van Wingerden's floating farm held thirty-two cows, with a maximum capacity of forty. Van Wingerden hopes that the model may be adapted for other urban areas to reduce the cost and pollution from transporting dairy products to cities.

Rotterdam is only one of many cities beginning to realize the need for far-reaching adaptation techniques. More communities are developing ways to deal with changed weather patterns and increasing environmental threats. But this was not always so.

MORAL IMPERATIVE

As public awareness of climate change grew in the 1990s, little attention was focused on ways to cope with its effects. Instead, scientists and activists called for a lowering of greenhouse gas emissions to halt climate change and lessen its effects. This approach is called mitigation. Adaptation, sometimes called resilience, is an approach that develops ways to live with climate change, to make the best of an already deteriorating situation. But to some individuals, talk of adaptation seemed like an easy and dangerous out. They believed it might encourage a false confidence that things weren't so bad after all. If people found ways to cope with climate change, they might be slow to change their energy-consuming habits or to confront the seriousness of the crisis. Even former vice president Al Gore called adaptation "a kind of laziness" in his 1992 best-selling book *Earth in the Balance*. He believed that we should beat climate change—not learn to live with it.

But carbon emission continued to rise. By the second decade of the twenty-first century, climate change was already apparent in the severity of weather events, melting glaciers, floods, and droughts. According to the authors of the "Trajectories" paper, even humanity's best efforts will not be enough to stop all climate change. Although hopeful that a stabilized Earth can still be achieved, the authors caution that humanity must find ways to deal with a very changed planet.

Experts agree that mitigation and adaptation are both essential in dealing with climate change. In 2013 Gore published another book, *The Future*. This time, he talked about the "moral imperative" to develop adaptation strategies and to curb carbon emissions. The World

Bank also supports both approaches and has announced a $10 billion a year investment in climate adaptation for 2019 to 2024. "Our new plan will put climate resilience on an equal footing with our investment in a low carbon future for the first time," then World Bank CEO Kristalina Georgieva said in a press release in January 2019. "We will ramp up our funding to help people build a more resilient future, especially the poorest and most vulnerable who are most affected."

BANGLADESH: YOU'RE GOING TO HAVE TO LEARN FROM US

Threatened by melting glaciers in the northern area and rising sea levels in the southern area, the low-lying country of Bangladesh is at especially high risk from climate change. Already disruption in rain patterns may leave one area in a drought, while another suffers heavy downpours. During the rainy season, a fifth of the nation can be underwater. In 2009 Cyclone Aila ravaged the country, destroying homes and flooding farmlands and rice paddies with salty water. In Bangladesh 113 people died and almost 500,000 were forced into shelters. When they were able to return home, their traditional crops would not grow in the salty ground.

Many homes are destroyed in Bangladesh each year as rising water levels cause erosion on river banks and coastlines. Not only does erosion destroy houses and shelters, but it also makes farming difficult as crops may not be able to grow in the soil or are destroyed by high tides.

CLIMATE HERO ELIZABETH ENGLISH: THERE HAD TO BE A BETTER WAY

Canadian architect Elizabeth English was studying at Louisiana State University's Hurricane Center when Hurricane Katrina hit New Orleans in 2005. Winds of over 70 miles (113 km) per hour tore roofs off houses and hurled debris through windows. The plight of thousands of people forced from their homes by raging floods saddened English greatly. Afterward, she also became upset by the government's response to the disaster. Federal officials wanted to relocate some communities entirely, a measure English thought was unfair and unnecessary. Some officials advised residents in low-lying areas to elevate their homes' foundations or to raise their homes on stilts. English felt this scheme would make it difficult for neighbors to get to know one another and socialize. It would destroy the sense of community. "There had to be a better way," she told the *New Yorker* magazine in 2018.

English turned to amphibious architecture as the better climate adaptation strategy. She devised a way to fit "buoyancy blocks" made of foam onto the foundations of existing homes. In the event of flooding, the houses rise and float on the water. As the waters

The Kompong Luong Floating Village in Cambodia is one of the largest floating villages in the world. The houses are mostly houseboats that can be moved from place to place on the lake. One of the dangers of living on the lake is being capsized when large motorboats pass. Therefore, residents are careful to keep their homes close to the shore.

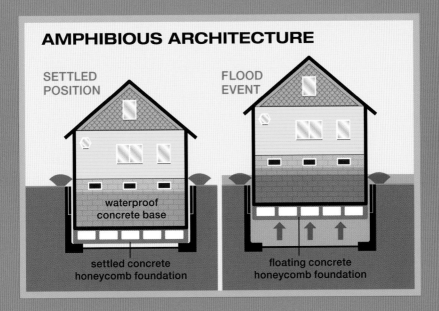

AMPHIBIOUS ARCHITECTURE

SETTLED POSITION

FLOOD EVENT

waterproof concrete base

settled concrete honeycomb foundation

floating concrete honeycomb foundation

recede, homes settle down on posts that anchor them to the ground. With her colleagues at the Buoyant Foundation Project, the nonprofit organization that she founded in 2006, English has designed homes for low-income, flood-prone areas of Jamaica and Nicaragua. She has worked with indigenous peoples in Canada and Louisiana. Interest in amphibious architecture continues to grow, although the concept has yet to be endorsed by the Federal Emergency Management Agency (FEMA). Federal insurance agencies and mortgage companies have also placed restrictions on amphibious houses. English realizes that her concept will not work in all cases—especially in areas where rapidly moving surges of water might be expected. "This is not a one-size-fits-all solution," she says. "But it's an excellent solution for some circumstances."

Funds from the World Bank enabled farmers to plant new crops that could thrive in a high-salt environment. They began to raise shrimp, crabs, and other salt-water seafood. Where floods eroded the soil, leaving barren, nonfertile land, they filled the area with compost and grew pumpkins. Because pumpkins can be preserved, farmers could sell them throughout the year. Fresh drinking water was another problem. To ensure an adequate supply, villagers began collecting rainwater. Several nongovernmental organizations supplied water tanks and desalination equipment for making salty water drinkable.

Between 2009 and 2019, however, natural disasters forced almost seven hundred thousand Bangladeshis a year to leave their communities. Most ended up in big-city slums, especially the capital city of Dhaka. Saleemul Huq, director of the country's International Centre for Climate Change and Development, hopes this cycle of poverty will stop with the growth of climate resilient, migrant-friendly secondary cities, such as Mongla on the southwestern coast. Such cities will combine seawalls and other safety measures with job opportunities, affordable houses, good schools, and hospitals. Residents of Mongla are protected by two flood-control gates. The city boasts a loudspeaker system to warn people of approaching bad weather and a water treatment plant that ensures half the population has running water in their homes.

In an imaginative but urgent climate change warning, Huq likened his country's struggles to the sudden arrival of extraterrestrials: "It's as if the initial scout ships of the alien invasion have landed on Earth, and one of them has landed in Bangladesh. The mother ship's on its way. When it comes it's going to land in New York, London, Paris. You guys are not ready for it [climate change] yet. But you're going to have to learn from us how to deal with it. Because we are learning."

ROBOTS AND ARTIFICIAL INTELLIGENCE

When soaring temperatures and drought make it dangerous to work outdoors, can robots take over for farmers in the field? Some researchers think so. Scientists from Israel, the Netherlands, Sweden, and Belgium have developed a massive-looking robot, named Sweeper, that can recognize yellow peppers, determine if they are ripe, harvest them with a small razor, and drop them into a basket. Other companies have plans for robots that pick strawberries, tomatoes, or cotton. But robots have many other roles on the land and in the ocean. Robots with artificial intelligence (AI) can use specialized sensors to monitor the health and growth rate of different plant species. This helps farmers decide which crops are most resistant to heat and drought and gives them a better chance of a successful harvest.

Artificial intelligence also shows special promise in helping researchers assess damage after weather catastrophes like Hurricane Maria in 2017. A report by several leaders in artificial intelligence described other ways that smart technologies can help deal with climate changes. These include the following:

1. Make the delivery of electricity more efficient so that little or no energy is wasted.
2. Improve the performance of electric vehicles.
3. Monitor environmental factors to automatically adjust the heating and cooling systems of buildings.
4. Use satellite imagery to evaluate greenhouse gas emissions from agricultural practices.
5. Develop low-carbon alternatives to steel and concrete.
6. Predict severe weather events with a greater degree of accuracy.

James Hodson is the CEO of AI for Good, which researches ways to apply artificial intelligence to world problems. "When we get more people involved in machine learning (a form of AI) to tackle these problems, it's more likely we'll find solutions." But artificial intelligence can't do it all. Hodson also stresses the need for "social solutions—the way we lead our lives, spend government money and the ways we force corporations to act better."

RAISING AN ISLAND: A DAUNTING TASK

As president of the Marshall Islands, Hilda Heine has overseen important climate adaptations—building up coastlines; strengthening roads, bridges, and other structures; and finding ways to make food and water more secure. But it is not enough. In the face of worsening floods and a prediction that the islands could be totally submerged by 2050, Heine made an unprecedented announcement. "Raising our islands is a daunting task but one that must be done," she said in 2019. To save their country, Marshall Islanders may have to dredge a lagoon, using the reclaimed earth, silt, and sand to build up the rest of the island.

Although the nation will continue to push for lower carbon emissions, Chief Secretary Ben Graham reiterates the need to focus more attention on resilience and adaptation strategies, both at home and in all countries. He hopes that the world's other atoll nations, Kiribati, Tuvalu, and the Maldives, will come together to discuss ideas, secure donations, and enlist the help of international organizations. "We are the only nations in the world who now face real prospects of being completely wiped off the map," Graham said, "so we need accelerated support for adaptation from our major partners."

SPONGE CITIES

Technological solutions can do a great deal to buffer the effects of climate change, but nature also has a crucial role to play. Cities recognize this when they combine gray infrastructure such as seawalls or tunnels with green infrastructure, or nature-based solutions to climate mitigation and adaptation. One example of "green infrastructure" is the use of open lands and vegetation to absorb rainwater and reduce the chance of flooding. China's Sponge City Initiative, launched in 2015, seeks to lessen the accumulation of rainwater in sixteen cities through a more efficient use of nature. The solutions include parks, wetlands, and green rooftops covered

TOKYO'S UNDERGROUND TEMPLE

Climate change is increasing the frequency and intensity of storms in Japan. Tokyo, parts of which are below sea level, is especially at risk. The city and surrounding area's thirty-eight million residents are also at risk for earthquakes and tsunamis. A 2014 study by a Swiss insurance firm labeled Tokyo and the nearby port of Yokohama "the riskiest metropolitan area in the world." To prepare for possible disasters, Japan built the enormous underground water drainage facility in Kasukabe, just north of Tokyo. Completed in 2009, the facility collects overflow from the city's waterways in enormous silos. At 83 feet tall (25 m) and 580 feet long (177 m), supported by giant pillars, the main container is so vast that it's called the Underground Temple. Water flows from the tanks through almost 4 miles (6.4 km) of tunnels before it is pumped into the Edo River. The largest such system in the world, the tunnels are able to transport 200 tons (181 t) of water per second.

"We're preparing for flooding beyond anything we've seen," said Kuniharu Abe, the facility's chief, in 2017. "Until now, at least, we've been successful."

A look at the inside of the Metropolitan Area Outer Underground Discharge Channel in Kasukabe, Saitama, Japan, that is also known as Ryukyukan, G-Can, or the Underground Temple.

This model of a sponge city was displayed at the 2018 China International Import Expo in Shanghai, China. The model features examples of permeable walkways as well as showing the underground tanks that would hold excess water.

with vegetation that absorbs water. Special permeable pavements merge the benefits of both technology and nature, providing sturdy surfaces that are also porous. During storms, water tends to accumulate on paved areas because it has nowhere else to go. But permeable roads and walkways hold surplus water like a sponge so that it does not run off and contribute to flooding. In 2018 Nanganqu Park in the Chinese city of Wuhan became a model sponge site with wetlands, ponds, rain gardens, and permeable walkways. Excess water seeps through these natural elements into underground tunnels or tanks. The water remains stored when levels in the nearby river run high and is released when the river's level returns to normal.

Liao Baozheng, a retired electrical engineer, appreciates the way the park contributes to his city's quality of life. "The air is always fresh here (in the park)," he said in 2019. "In Wuhan's scorching summer, it's cooler here as the lush vegetation brings down the temperature by two or three degrees."

Sponge environments show such promise that cities in other parts of the world are starting to notice. For example, Berlin, Germany, is also looking to lessen the effects of climate change through permeable paving, moss and grass covered rooftops, and urban wetlands.

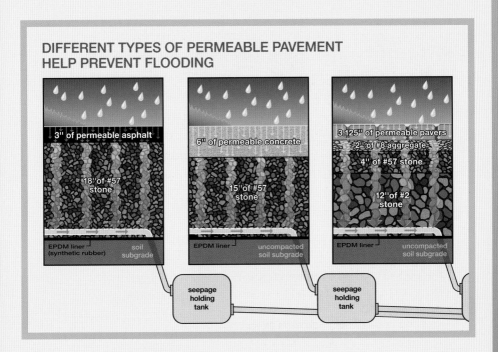

DIFFERENT TYPES OF PERMEABLE PAVEMENT HELP PREVENT FLOODING

3" of permeable asphalt

18" of #57 stone

EPDM liner (synthetic rubber)   soil subgrade

6" of permeable concrete

15" of #57 stone

EPDM liner   uncompacted soil subgrade

3.125" of permeable pavers

2" of #8 aggregate

4" of #57 stone

12" of #2 stone

EPDM liner   uncompacted soil subgrade

seepage holding tank

seepage holding tank

Low-impact development, a term used in the United States and Canada, depends on similar techniques.

A YEAR OF ACTION

Support for climate resilience got a boost in October 2018 with the creation of the Global Commission on Adaptation. Headed by former UN secretary-general Ban Ki-moon, World Bank CEO Kristalina Georgieva, and Microsoft cofounder Bill Gates, the commission is also composed of twenty-five world leaders and seventeen countries, including China, India, South Africa, Germany, Mexico, and Canada. Although the United States is not officially a member, Francis Suarez, the mayor of Miami joined the commission. Miami has already experienced severe flooding from rising tides and heavy rains.

After a year of researching ways to ensure climate resilience, the commission presented its best plans at the United Nations Climate

Change Summit in September 2019. The summit marked the beginning of a "year of action" to introduce the adaptation strategies throughout the world. Their investigation highlighted five key areas in need of improvement: 1) early-warning systems to alert people of approaching hurricanes and typhoons, 2) stronger infrastructure such as better roads, bridges, and protections against storm surges, 3) improved agriculture practices, 4) enhancement of mangrove forests to store carbon and protect coastlines, and 5) plans to protect the water supply in the face of extreme weather events and climate change.

MANGROVES: MITIGATION AND ADAPTATION

Resilient tropical mangroves with dense, tangled roots and branches cover many coastal areas and provide a barrier against storm surges and violent waves. Studies have shown that mangroves helped minimize coastal damage from the Indian Ocean tsunami in 2004 and from Hurricane Wilma in 2005. Mangroves also shield the Kennedy Space Center at Cape Canaveral, Florida. Besides sheltering land, they are also extremely efficient in absorbing CO_2 and other greenhouse gases and storing them in the soil, thereby lessening the effects of climate change.

With warming temperatures, mangroves have begun to migrate north of their traditional habitat in the tropics and into temperate zones in the Americas, Africa, Asia, and Australia. But human interference, particularly clearing coastal lands to facilitate fish and seafood farming, has led to a decline in the number of mangrove forests. Research indicates that 35 percent of the world's mangrove environment was destroyed between 1980 and 2000. According to one estimate, mangrove forests throughout the world are being lost three to five times faster than other forests. Protecting and restoring these forests not only helps communities deal with the effects of severe weather, but it also helps mitigate climate change itself.

According to the commission, an investment of $1.8 trillion to further these goals would save $7.1 trillion in the long run.

Although some economists and scientists predict that adaptation measures could cost $500 billion a year by 2050, Ban Ki-moon is optimistic. "The money can be mobilized," he said. "If there is a political will, I think we can handle this matter."

"Our climate has already changed," Georgieva said in 2018. "We face a choice: business as usual and hope for the best. Or we can act now and build for a resilient future."

CHAPTER EIGHT

YOUNG PEOPLE MAKING THEIR VOICES HEARD

"Unlike you, my generation will not give up without a fight." Seventeen-year-old Greta Thunberg directed this resolute pledge to representatives to the World Economic Forum at Davos, Switzerland, in 2020. Political, business, and industrial leaders from 117 countries focused on the teenager as she proceeded to list her nonnegotiable demands:

"Immediately halt all investments in fossil fuel exploration and extraction. Immediately end all fossil fuel subsidies. And immediately and completely divest from fossil fuels. We don't want these things done by 2050, 2030 or even 2021. We want this done now."

Thunberg went on to stress the right of young people to inherit a habitable and ecologically balanced Earth. "I wonder what will you tell your children was the reason to fail and leave them facing a climate chaos you knowingly brought upon them. . . . We are telling you to act as if you loved your children above all else." With these challenging words, Greta concluded her remarks to some of the world's most powerful people.

SCHOOL STRIKE FOR CLIMATE CHANGE

Less than a year and a half earlier, Greta had been an unknown ninth-grade student in Stockholm, Sweden. She had first learned about climate change when she was eight years old. The news that man-made activities had precipitated an environmental crisis shocked her. She couldn't get the developing catastrophe out of her mind. It was one of the reasons she fell into a depression several years later. She talked to her parents continually about climate change. She showed them reports, films, and pictures. Finally, she managed to convince them that a very real, very serious crisis existed. Her mother, a celebrated opera singer, stopped flying—

Greta Thunberg speaks at a climate change protest in Lausanne, Switzerland, in January 2020 before the Davos World Economic Forum.

even though that cut back on her opportunities to perform. Her father became a vegetarian. Greta decided that if she could change her parents' lives, she might be able to change other people's lives too.

When students in Parkland, Florida, walked out of class to call attention to the need for gun control legislation, Greta took note. Stoneman Douglas High School had lost seventeen people in a horrific mass shooting in February 2018. The students would do anything they could to prevent such a tragedy from ever happening again.

Inspired by the Parkland students, Greta skipped school on August 20, 2018, and rode her bike to the Swedish Parliament House. She positioned herself on the steps with a sign she had painted reading, "SKOLSTREJK FOR KLIMATET" (School Strike for Climate). When she returned the next day, people began joining her protest. Greta went on strike from school every day until Sweden held its national elections on September 9. By then her protest had gained so much momentum that she was asked to speak at a rally of the People's Climate March. Thousands of people would be present. Greta, who has been diagnosed with Asperger's, a mild form of autism, was not used to speaking in public. Her parents were concerned that making a speech might prove too stressful. But Greta refused to be dissuaded. She views her Asperger's as a strength. "If I had been just like everyone else and been social, then I would have just tried to start an organization," she said in 2019. "But I couldn't do that. I'm not very good with people, so I did something with myself instead."

Greta's speech at the rally was only the beginning. In December 2018, she traveled by train to Poland where she spoke before the UN Climate Change Conference. The next month she spoke at the World Economic Forum in Davos, Switzerland. She embarked on a speaking tour through Europe that included a meeting with Pope Francis. By May 2019, Greta appeared on the cover of *Time* magazine, and 612,000 people were following her on Twitter. She continued to put her message forward through school strikes every Friday.

AN INTERNATIONAL MOVEMENT

Greta's example prompted other young people to act. Her "School Strike for Climate" sign has been translated into languages all over the world. On March 15, 2019, tens of thousands of students in 112 countries walked out of class in the first global school climate strike. Governments and organizations noticed. The strike is credited with helping to provoke demonstrations in London by Extinction Rebellion, a nonviolent movement that demands immediate action to halt the loss of plant and animal species and the possible extinction of the human race. Under pressure to act, the United Kingdom and Ireland declared climate emergencies. A parliamentary committee in the UK advised the country to set a goal of zero greenhouse gas emissions by 2050. Angela Merkel, chancellor of Germany, also said that the school strikes helped convince her that the European Union should end emissions by 2050.

Meanwhile, the Fridays for Future campaign continued, with students in twenty-five countries showing unity with Greta's goals by striking on Fridays. In May 2019, young people held another mass event in which students from twenty-three hundred schools in over 130 countries went on strike.

Three months later, Thunberg sailed to the United States on a small, emissions-free boat. Ultimately, she planned to attend COP25 in Santiago, Chile. But first, she joined in climate protests across the nation from New York to Los Angeles. In September she spoke before the US Congress, giving them a copy of the 2018 IPCC report on global warming. She told congresspersons not to listen to her but to focus on what the scientists were saying.

Then she traveled to New York where she participated in another demonstration as four million people across the globe also marched in what may have been the largest climate protest to date. She gave a particularly scathing address to the United Nations Action Summit. After reiterating the human suffering and deaths caused by the climate

CLIMATE HERO AUTUMN PELTIER: WATER IS A BASIC HUMAN RIGHT

Autumn Peltier was traveling with her family to an indigenous people's water ceremony in Canada when she came across a sign warning that all water must be boiled. Members of the Wikwemikong First Nation,

In January 2020, Autumn Peltier participated in the World Economic Forum in Davos, Switzerland.

Peltier's parents had taught her the importance of protecting water. She asked what the puzzling sign meant.

Autumn's mother explained that many First Nation (indigenous) communities did not have access to safe drinking water and were forced to boil their water. "One day it really affected me and I actually cried about it," she told the Canadian Broadcast Corporation. It was a turning point for Autumn who began defending everyone's right to enjoy clean water. She was only eight years old.

Four years later, in 2016, Peltier was chosen to present Canadian prime minister Justin Trudeau with a traditional copper bowl from the indigenous population. "When I came face-to-face with him something came over me," she later recalled. "I just told him I was very unhappy with the broken promises he made to my people." She was referring specifically to his support of pipelines that jeopardize indigenous communities and can contaminate their drinking water.

As chief water commissioner for the Anishinabek Nation, an advocacy group for indigenous peoples in Ontario, Peltier continues to push for clean drinking water. In 2018 she spoke about water rights to the UN General Assembly in New York. "Water is a basic human right," she declared. After founding Mother Earth Water Walk, she walked 15,000 miles (24,140 km) along the shores of the Great Lakes to call attention to the need for safe drinking water for everyone. "There are a lot of youth that are standing up and it's because we're really seeing the effects of climate change," she said in 2019. "A lot of us youth are scared. We are wondering do we even have a future to look forward to."

crisis, the end of ecosystems, and the looming specter of mass extinctions, she accused world leaders of focusing their attention on money and false economics. "We will not let you get away with this," she said. After the speech, Greta made an official complaint with fifteen other young people from across the globe. Filed under the 1989 UN Convention on the Rights of the Child, the complaint states that climate change threatens children's rights to health and a peaceful world.

THE FORCE OF ANGRY KIDS

When unrest in Chile caused the COP25 to be moved to Madrid, Spain, Thunberg faced a dilemma. Stranded on the wrong side of the Atlantic, she refused to lengthen her carbon footprint by flying to the conference. An Australian couple with a 48-foot-long (15 m) environmentally friendly boat came to her rescue. Arriving in Portugal three days before the conference, she told reporters, "I think people are underestimating the force of angry kids. If they want us to stop being angry, then maybe they should stop making us angry."

On September 20, 2019, three days before the UN Climate Action Summit, close to 250,000 students in New York gathered for a climate strike. Worldwide, over 4 million people took part in the strike, which was one of the largest protests for action on climate change in history.

The next week at COP25, Thunberg decided not to use the powerful expressions she had in the past, such as "Our house is on fire," or "How dare you." She said that people tend to concentrate on such compelling phrases instead of the facts and science of climate

CLIMATE HERO JAMIE MARGOLIN: ZERO HOUR

When she was fifteen, two environmental disasters prompted Jamie Margolin to take a stand for climate action and for social justice. Hurricane Maria devastated Puerto Rico, and wildfires in Canada raged out of control. Jamie was deeply troubled that Puerto Ricans weren't getting the help and financial aid they desperately needed. She was upset that smoke from the fires drifted into her home state of Washington, making it difficult to breathe. Believing that young people could make a difference, she helped found the youth climate action group Zero Hour in 2017. Jamie, who is of Hispanic descent, and the other women of color who lead the organization have strong views about how to deal with environmental issues. They do not believe that "slapping a solar panel on the climate crisis" is enough. "We tackle climate change from an intersectional lens," Jamie told *Teen Vogue* in 2018. "And we believe that the people who feel the worst effects of an issue are the experts and must be at the forefront of the issues solutions," she said, "and the majority of those people are people of color. That's not a coincidence."

With other teenagers who helped establish Zero Hour, Jamie held a large youth protest march in Washington, DC, in July 2018. Undeterred by rain, hundreds of young people from all over the country shouted slogans as they marched such as "Water is life," and "Take it to the streets. Take it to the polls."

One year later, Jamie and her coleaders chose Miami as the site of a youth climate summit. Threatened by rising sea levels and heat waves, the city is home to many low-income residents and minorities who suffer disproportionately from what is happening. "There is no time for us to grow up and save the world later," said Jamie. "It's now or never. . . . Young people's power depends on our ability to influence the people in power. Why are they not taking action now?"

change itself. She reminded wealthy nations of their responsibilities to reduce emissions and to help poorer nations. "We do not have to wait," she said. "We can start the change right now."

For her part in setting off an international youth movement, Greta was nominated for the Nobel Peace Prize in 2019. Although she did not win, she did receive the Right Livelihood Award. Greta used the prize money to create a nonprofit organization called the Greta Thunberg Foundation aimed at advancing environmental and social sustainability and furthering education on mental health. Greta was also chosen as *Time*'s Person of the Year for 2019.

JULIANA V. UNITED STATES: KIDS GO TO COURT

School strikes are not the whole story. Young people have also taken the fight for climate action to court. *Juliana v. United States*, a lawsuit filed in 2015 in Eugene, Oregon, on behalf of twenty-one children, then ages eight to nineteen, asks the courts to stop the government from using fossil fuels and from supporting the fossil fuel industry. In the words of one federal judge, "This is no ordinary lawsuit." Kelsey Juliana, the lead plaintiff, now a young adult, especially worries about droughts and wildfires and the health risks they pose.

Julia Olson, the plaintiffs' lawyer and chief legal counsel of the nonprofit group Our Children's Trust, solicited the children from environmental groups in many parts of the country. The case she put together claims that the federal government has a responsibility to safeguard the nation's environment and that it has failed to do so. It provides documentation that government officials knew about the devastating consequences of climate change as early as 1965. "Every president [since Lyndon Johnson] knew that burning fossil fuels was causing climate change," Olson told the news program *60 Minutes* in 2019. The plaintiffs (those filing the suit) want the courts to order the government to get the nation off fossil fuels by 2050.

Although the right to a "stable climate system" is not mentioned in the Constitution, the case alleges that the Fifth and Ninth Amendments guarantee the right. The Fifth Amendment states that no one shall be "deprived of life, liberty, or property, without due process of law." And yet rising seas, droughts, floods, fires, and extreme weather, caused or exacerbated by climate change, are threatening those very rights.

The Ninth Amendment reads, "The enumeration in the Constitution of certain rights shall not be construed to deny or disparage others retained by the people." So a right may exist even though it is not specifically mentioned in the Constitution.

The federal government, however, does not accept such arguments and has tried to have the case dismissed. It believes that it's up to Congress—not the courts—to take action on climate change. In November 2016, two days after Trump was elected president, the

Juliana v. United States plaintiff Vic Barrett testified at a joint hearing of the House Foreign Affairs Subcommittee on Europe, Eurasia, Energy, and the Environment and the House Select Committee on the Climate Crisis in Washington, DC, alongside Greta Thunberg and other youth activists. On September 18, 2019, representatives from the US government gathered to listen to the testimonies of notable youth leaders like Vic and Greta.

plaintiffs achieved a major victory when federal judge Ann Aiken of the District of Oregon ruled that the case could go forward. But on January 17, 2020, a three-judge panel of the Ninth Circuit Court of Appeals sided with the government in a 2–1 decision. While acknowledging that the plaintiffs made a powerful case for climate action, the court ruled that it did not have the constitutional power to force the federal government to meet their demands.

Judge Josephine L. Staton disagreed in a strongly worded dissent. "Where is the hope in today's decision?" she wrote. "Plaintiffs' claims are based on science. . . . If plaintiffs' fears, backed by the government's own studies, prove true, history will not judge us kindly. When seas envelop our coastal cities, fires and droughts haunt our interiors, and storms ravage everything between, those remaining will ask: Why did so many do so little?"

But the children and their lawyer have not given up. "We will continue this case because only the courts can help us," twelve-year-old Levi Draheim said after the ruling. "We firmly believe the courts can vindicate our constitutional rights and we will not stop until we get a decision that says so."

EVERYDAY CLIMATE COURAGE

Every day people deal with the effects of climate change, and every day they can take small but courageous steps to do something about it. As young people think about reducing their carbon footprints, they can focus on four critical areas: food, transportation, energy, and politics.

FOOD

The world population is growing and expected to reach 9.7 billion by 2050. A way must be found to feed everyone without razing more forests or draining more wetlands. The food must reach people without contributing to greenhouse gas emissions. Environmental experts tell us that this is possible. Smart decisions on the part of consumers can help.

Here are some suggestions for teenagers and adults:

1. **EAT LESS MEAT.** Some experts believe this is the single most important thing you can do to fight climate change. When woodlands are razed to make way for livestock, important carbon sinks are destroyed and wild animals lose their natural habitat. And cows emit large amounts of methane. Climate scientists warn that consumption of beef must decrease by 90 percent in industrialized nations to stop the climate crisis.

2. **EAT SEASONALLY AND BUY LOCALLY.** Food grown or produced locally does not carry the heavy carbon footprint of food that has been transported long distances. Farmers' markets and backyard gardens are good for the environment.

3. **REDUCE WASTE BY COMPOSTING.** Vegetable peelings, eggshells, and coffee grounds can be used to enrich your soil.

4. **REUSE.** Bring your own recyclable bags to the grocery store. Buy eco-friendly products, and recycle packaging as much as possible.

TRANSPORTATION

The Center for Sustainable Systems at the University of Michigan says that the average passenger car releases 0.8 pounds (0.4 kg) of carbon dioxide for every mile (1.6 km) it drives. In 2016, cars and lightweight trucks were responsible for 1.2 billion tons (1.1 billion t) of CO_2 emissions in the United States, or 17 percent of the country's total emissions. Individuals can make meaningful differences in curbing these emissions. Here are just a few ideas:

1. **DRIVE LESS.** Carpooling cuts down on traffic jams and unhealthy pollution as well as fights climate change. Walk

when possible, or use public transportation. Where it's safe, bike to your destination.

2. **DRIVE WISELY.** Driving an energy-efficient vehicle and not exceeding speed limits also cut back on emissions.

3. **FLY LESS.** The amount of CO_2 emitted by planes depends on the type of aircraft, the weight it carries, and the duration of the journey. The 2016 average emissions for domestic flights in the United States was 0.4 pounds (0.2 kg) of CO_2 per passenger mile (1.6 km). Flying less makes good environmental sense.

ENERGY

Solar panels aren't the only way to generate clean electricity for your home. Your parents may know that 50 percent of customers in the US have the option to buy renewable energy directly from their power companies, according to the Department of Energy. Renewable energy certificates, which are available for everyone to purchase, are another

Many cities have worked to make public transportation more eco-friendly. Hybrid electric buses run on both gas and electricity, which reduces the emissions made by burning fossil fuels such as gasoline. These buses are also more efficient because their engines weigh less than a traditional gas-powered vehicle.

way to support the generation of green power. Meanwhile, careful monitoring of your daily use of electricity can help the environment and lessen carbon footprints. Following just a few simple steps at home can make a difference:

1. **USE LED LIGHT BULBS.** These bulbs use 75 percent less electricity than other bulbs and last about twenty-five times longer.
2. **TURN LIGHTS OFF WHEN YOU LEAVE A ROOM.**
3. **UNPLUG ELECTRONIC DEVICES SUCH AS SCANNERS AND PRINTERS WHEN NOT IN USE.** Even when they're turned off, some devices use small amounts of energy. The amount of electricity used by inactive electronics in a year equals the output of twelve power plants.
4. **WASH DISHES AND CLOTHES IN COLD WATER.** This saves the energy required to heat the water.
5. **REDUCE, REUSE, RECYCLE.** The ways to live this popular maxim are only limited by your imagination. How people live their daily lives can make a crucial difference.

POLITICS

Author of several important books on climate change, including the classic *An Inconvenient Truth*, Al Gore has written of two types of tipping points. An "environmental tipping point" releases enormous amounts of greenhouse gases, causes ecological disaster, and accelerates climate change. A "political tipping point" refers to the momentum that is reached when enough people make climate action their top priority. "I think we're really close to that political threshold, where it is not as partisan, where people start competing to offer the best solutions," Gore said in 2019. He sees great hope in the growing youth movement and organizations.

SUNRISE MOVEMENT

Founded in 2017 by a dozen people in their twenties, the Sunrise Movement has rapidly grown into a major force for climate action and a Green New Deal. Its members, who come from many ethnic and religious groups, believe that climate issues are closely related to issues of social and economic justice. Often they sing during protests. Representative Alexandria Ocasio-Cortez, who supports their nonviolent protests, has described the Green New Deal as "a historic opportunity to virtually eliminate poverty in the United States."

The Sunrise Movement continued to push for the Green New Deal more vigorously than ever after its rejection by the Senate in 2019. Sunrise held two hundred town hall meetings throughout the country within a month. They wound up the whirlwind tour at Howard University in Washington, DC, where they were joined by Ocasio-Cortez and Democratic presidential hopeful Bernie Sanders. Varshini Prakash, a cofounder of Sunrise, addressed an audience of fifteen hundred students and activists. She spoke of her home in East Boston, which is endangered by rising sea levels. She also spoke of her family's roots in India, "a place that has been completely devastated by the climate crisis." And she spoke of a million people in India displaced by catastrophic weather. "I'm here," she declared, "because I believe that no person should ever have to live in fear of losing the people that they love or the places that they call home due to crises that are preventable."

There are always ways to make your voice heard:

1. **ASK YOUR SCHOOL TO PROMOTE CLIMATE EDUCATION AND TO INVESTIGATE WAYS TO LESSEN THE SCHOOL'S CARBON FOOTPRINT.** Ideas might include installing recycling bins, composting plant waste from the cafeteria, or raising money to install solar panels.

2. **PARTICIPATE IN LOCAL YOUTH CLIMATE EVENTS.**

3. **WHEN YOU ARE OLD ENOUGH TO VOTE, VOTE FOR CANDIDATES WITH STRONG POLICIES FOR CLIMATE ACTION.** Even before you're able to vote, you can write to your congressperson demanding that he or she support legislation to lower emissions and protect the environment.

STILL IN HUMANITY'S GRASP

Greta Thunberg believes that many people still remain ignorant of the looming climate catastrophe. Her mission is to call attention to what is happening. As people acquire understanding, they support measures to save the environment. "We aren't destroying the biosphere because we are selfish," she said. "We are doing it simply because we are unaware. I think that is very hopeful, because once we know, once we realize, then we change, then we act."

In late 2019 and early 2020, the novel coronavirus SARS-CoV-2 caused an outbreak of COVID-19 cases that threatened and continues to threaten the health of people across the globe. Many businesses suspended operations and people avoided unnecessary travel in an effort to halt the threat. By September 4, 2020, the New York Times reported more than 26.3 million known cases and over 869,000 deaths worldwide. Although the urgency of the pandemic crisis understandably eclipsed climate change in the headlines, many researchers see a link between the two crises. While pollution does not increase the risk of contracting the coronavirus, a Harvard study indicates that high levels of pollution does increase the risk of death from the coronavirus. Low-income families and minorities are the hardest hit, facing greater health risks and financial hardship from both the climate crisis and the coronavirus.

Many scientists and environmentalists urged governments to take ecological impacts into consideration after the pandemic. Declines in greenhouse gases due to the industrial and transportation slowdowns cannot halt the climate crisis. But they can motivate people to work toward further reductions. "We will not—we cannot—go back to the way things were," Tedros Adhanom Ghebreyesus, director-general of the World Health Organization (WHO), said in August 2020. "Throughout history, outbreaks and pandemics have changed economies and societies. This one will be no different. In particular, the pandemic has given new impetus to the need to accelerate efforts to respond to climate change." The "Manifesto for a Healthy and Green Recovery," published by the WHO, lists six directives for achieving a healthier and sustainable future: protecting nature, creating safe water supplies and sanitation systems, lessening dependence on fossil fuels, supporting sustainable and healthy food systems, constructing resilient cities, and ending subsidies on fossil fuels.

Only a global commitment to put Earth's ecological balance first will be sufficient to stop the climate crisis and to ensure a healthier future for everyone. Climate courage requires those in developed nations to prioritize the well-being of the planet over an easy or privileged lifestyle. It challenges leaders in less developed countries to improve life for their citizens without greatly increasing their greenhouse gases. A stabilized Earth is still in humanity's grasp—if enough people are willing to fight for it.

SOME HIGHLIGHTS OF CLIMATE CHANGE DEVELOPMENT

1800s   The Industrial Revolution depends on fossil fuels to power factories and railroads, thereby adding to the amount of greenhouse gases in the atmosphere.

1957   David Keeling begins measurements of atmospheric CO_2 at the Mauna Loa Observatory in Hawaii.

1969   The publication of the photograph, *Earthrise*, helps start the environmental movement.

1970   The first Earth Day is celebrated on April 22nd.

1988   James Hansen's testimony before Congress brings climate change to the public's attention.

The United Nations sets up the Intergovernmental Panel on Climate Change (IPCC).

2005   The Kyoto Protocol takes effect.

2007   James Hansen declares that the maximum safe atmospheric level of CO_2 is 350 ppm, a figure that the world had already surpassed by over 30 ppm.

2008   The polar bear is listed as an endangered species.

2015   The United Nations adopts seventeen Sustainable Development Goals.

In the Paris Agreement, almost all nations agree to set targets to limit their carbon emissions and to report on their progress.

The lawsuit *Juliana v. United States* is filed on behalf of twenty-one children.

2017   President Trump announces his intention to withdraw the United States from the Paris Agreement.

The youth climate activist organizations the Sunrise Movement and Zero Hour are founded.

2018   The paper "Trajectories of the Earth System in the Anthropocene" calls upon humanity to assume a stewardship role toward the environment.

The IPCC reports that human activities release 42 billion tons (38 billion t) of CO_2 into the atmosphere each year.

2019   Alexandria Ocasio-Cortez introduces the Green New Deal into Congress. The Senate defeats it two months later.

Inspired by the actions of Greta Thunberg, the first global school strike for climate change takes place in March.

2020   *Juliana v. United States* is dismissed by the Ninth Circuit Court of Appeals.

The National Oceanic and Atmospheric Administration announces that the first month of 2020 was the hottest January on record.

A record temperature of 100.4°F (38°C) is measured in Siberia.

US House of Representatives Democrats release a Climate Crisis Action Plan calling for net-zero carbon emissions by 2050.

GLOSSARY

AMPHIBIOUS ARCHITECTURE: buildings that are designed or retrofitted to rise and float in the event of flooding

ANTHROPOCENE: a proposed geological epoch that is defined by the way humanity is changing the environment

BIODIVERSITY: the vast variety of plants and animals in Earth's biosphere

BIOFUEL: fuel that is derived from organic matter

BIOSPHERE: sections of Earth and the atmosphere that are inhabited by living organisms

CARBON CAPTURE: technology to remove excess carbon from the atmosphere

CARBON FOOTPRINT: a measure of the amount of CO_2 released into the atmosphere by a single individual over the course of a year, based on activities and lifestyle

CARBON SINK: natural areas, such as forests, wetlands, or oceans that absorb carbon dioxide from the air and store it

CLIMATE ADAPTATION: plans and schemes that help communities deal with the present and prepare for future effects of climate change

CLIMATE CHANGE: man-made changes to weather patterns and the environment due to an increase of carbon dioxide and other greenhouse gases in the atmosphere

CLIMATE MIGRANTS: individuals forced to leave their homes due to severe weather events or other effects of climate change such as rising ocean levels or drought

FOREST DIEBACK: the loss of wooded areas as trees and shrubs die out from the tips of their leaves or roots backward, due to a hostile environment or disease

FOSSIL FUELS: natural substances, such as gas or coal, that form over millennia from decayed plant and animal matter

GEOENGINEERING: use of technology to lessen the effects of climate change. The two main types of geoengineering are carbon capture and the deflection of solar radiation from Earth.

GLOBAL WARMING: the rise in world temperatures produced by greenhouse gases, emitted by human activities, into the atmosphere

GREENHOUSE GASES: gases such as carbon dioxide, methane water vapor, ozone, nitrous oxide, chlorofluorocarbons, and hydrofluorocarbons that hold heat in the atmosphere

GREEN NEW DEAL: legislation proposed in the United States that calls for sweeping measures to deal with climate change and bring about economic equality

HECTARE (Ha): a metric unit of square measure equal to 2.4711 acres or 11,960 square yards

HOTHOUSE EARTH: conditions in which global temperatures have soared beyond control and climate change is unstoppable. Large portions of Earth would become inhospitable to life in a hothouse Earth scenario.

ICE ALBEDO FEEDBACK: a positive feedback in which the melting of large amounts of reflective ice leads to darker patches on the ground and in the oceans that hold more heat

INDUSTRIAL REVOLUTION: the period beginning in the late eighteenth century when machines and engines that burn fossil fuels began to replace human labor in the production of goods

INTERSECTIONALITY: the ways that race, gender, and ethnicity overlap (or intersect), contributing to discrimination against minority groups or individuals

KEELING CURVE: a graph that shows the steady rise of CO_2 in the atmosphere (with seasonal variations) based on measurements taken at the Mauna Loa Observatory set up by Charles Keeling in 1958

KYOTO PROTOCOL: an international treaty requiring industrialized nations to set limits on CO_2 emissions. Signed in December 1997, it went into effect in February 2005.

MITIGATION: actions and strategies to reduce the effects of climate change

NEGATIVE FEEDBACK: a process that reduces initial warming as it relates to climate change

OCEAN ACIDIFICATION: an increasing acidity (decrease in pH) in oceans that is caused by absorption of CO_2 from the atmosphere and that is harmful to coral reefs and other marine life

PARIS CLIMATE AGREEMENT: an agreement that calls upon nations to reduce greenhouse emissions to keep global temperature below 3.6°F (2°C) above preindustrial levels and to develop ways to keep temperature increases within 2.7°F (1.5°C)

PERMAFROST: subsurface soil in the Arctic and Antarctic regions that remains frozen year-round and that contains a great deal of the greenhouse gas methane

PHOTOSYNTHESIS: when green plants create food from sunlight, CO_2, and water, releasing oxygen

POSITIVE FEEDBACK: a process that amplifies, or increases, the initial warming

SPONGE ENVIRONMENTS: areas in which the ground cover is specially cultivated to absorb excess water

STRATOSPHERIC AEROSOL INJECTION (SAI): a form of geoengineering in which particles sprayed into the atmosphere reflect the sun's radiation back into space

SUSTAINABILITY: the maintenance of an ecological balance without exhausting environmental resources; a natural resilience

TIPPING POINT: threshold beyond which the climate system will change radically

UNITED NATIONS FRAMEWORK CONVENTION ON CLIMATE CHANGE: an international treaty that set nonbinding limits on greenhouse gas emissions that was negotiated at the UN Earth Summit at Rio de Janeiro in 1992

SOURCE NOTES

4   Constance Okollet, "Change Is Killing Our People," *Guardian* (US edition), September 23, 2009, https://www.theguardian.com/commentisfree /cifamerica/2009/sep/22/united-nations-climate-change-uganda.

6   Wendy Becktold, "Ugandan Women Didn't Cause Climate Change, but They're Adapting to It," Sierra Club, October 12, 2017, https://www .sierraclub.org/sierra/2017-6-november-december/feature/ugandan-women -didnt-cause-climate-change-theyre-adapting-it.

7   Becktold.

7   Okollet, "Change."

11   Justin Worland, "Australia's Fires Are Terrifying. Will They Get World Leaders to Act on Climate Change?," *Time*, January 9, 2020, https://time .com/5762032/australia-fires-climate-change-world-leaders/.

11–12   Damian Carrington, "Extreme Global Weather Is the 'Face of Climate Change,' Says Leading Scientist," *Guardian* (US edition), July 27, 2018.

12   Joseph Stronbert, "What Is the Anthropocene and Are We in It?," *Smithsonian Magazine*, January 2013, https://www.smithsonianmag.com /science-nature/what-is-the-anthropocene-and-are-we-in-it-164801414/.

14   Will Steffen et al., "Planet at Risk of Heading towards 'Hothouse Earth' State," Stockholm Resilience Centre, August, 6, 2018, https://www .stockholmresilience.org/research/research-news/2018-08-06-planet-at-risk -of-heading-towards-hothouse-earth-state.html.

15   Sara Peach, "New 'Global Weirding' Series Informs, Entertains," Yale Climate Connections, November 21, 2016, https://www .yaleclimateconnections.org/2016/11/new-global-weirding-series -informs-entertains/.

15   Kate Yoder, "Is It Time to Retire 'Climate Change' for 'Climate Crisis?,'" Grist, June 17, 2019, https://grist.org/article/is-it-time-to-retire-climate -change-for-climate-crisis/.

15   Pam Wright, "Extreme Weather Events Have Greatest Likelihood of Threatening Human Existence, Experts Say," The Weather Channel, January 19, 2018, https://weather.com/science/environment/news/2018-01 -19-extreme-weather-threatens-human-existence.

16   Nadia Drake, "We Saw Earth Rise over the Moon in 1968. It Changed Everything," *National Geographic*, December 22, 2018, https://www .nationalgeographic.co.uk/space/2018/12/we-saw-earth-rise-over-moon -1968-it-changed-everything.

16   Ian Sample, "*Earthrise*: How the Iconic Image Changed the World," *Guardian* (US edition), December 24, 2018, https://www.theguardian.com /science/2018/dec/24/earthrise-how-the-iconic-image-changed-the-world.

16   NASA Content Administrator, editor, "Apollo Astronaut Shares Story of NASA's Earthrise Photo" *NASA*, March 29, 2012, updated August 7, 2017, accessed June 25, 2020, https://www.nasa.gov/centers/johnson/home/earthrise.html.

19   Sarah Emerson, "NASA Discovered a 'Disturbing' Glacier Hole Two-Thirds the Size of Manhattan, *Vice*, January 31, 2019, https://www.vice.com/en_us/article/9kpbgv/nasa-discovered-a-disturbing-glacier-hole-two-thirds-the-size-of-manhattan.

20   Will Steffen et al., "Trajectories of the Earth System in the Anthropocene," *Proceedings of the National Academy of Sciences* (PNAS) 115, no. 33, (August 14, 2018), pp. 8252-8259, accessed July 5, 2020, https://www.pnas.org/content/115/33/8252.

24   "Global Warming's Evil Twin: Ocean Acidification," Climate Reality Project, June 21, 2016, https://www.climaterealityproject.org/blog/global-warming-ocean-acidification.

26   Roxy Mathew Koll, "Up above the World So High, Climate Change Could Kill Some Clouds in the Sky," *Wire*, March 2, 2019, https://thewire.in/the-sciences/up-above-the-world-so-high-climate-change-could-kill-some-clouds-in-the-sky.

26   "High CO_2 Levels Can Destabilize Marine Layer Clouds," SpaceDaily, March 6, 2019, https://www.sciencedaily.com/releases/2019/02/190225123036.htm.

26   Yasemin Saplakoglu, "The Planet Is Dangerously Close to the Tipping Point for a 'Hothouse Earth," Live Science, August 6, 2018, https://www.livescience.com/63267-hothouse-earth-dangerously-close.html.

27   Brad Plumer, "Humans Are Speeding Extinction and Altering the Natural World at an Unprecedented Pace," *New York Times*, May 6, 2019, https://www.nytimes.com/2019/05/06/climate/biodiversity-extinction-united-nations.html.

27   Elizabeth Kolbert, "Climate Change and the New Age of Extinction," *New Yorker*, May 13, 2019, https://www.newyorker.com/magazine/2019/05/20/climate-change-and-the-new-age-of-extinction.

28   Josh Gabbatiss, "'Unprecedented Changes' Needed to Stop Global Warming as UN Report Reveals Islands Starting to Vanish and Coral Reefs Dying," *Independent* (London), October 8, 2018, https://www.independent.co.uk/environment/climate-change-ipcc-report-un-global-warming-15c-coral-reefs-arctic-ice-islands-incheon-korea-a8572926.html.

31   Bill McKibben, *Eaarth: Making a Life on a Tough New Planet* (New York: St. Martin's Griffin, 2010), 15.

31   Kendra Pierre-Louis, "Greenhouse Gas Emissions Accelerate like a 'Speeding Freight Train' in 2018," *New York Times*, December 5, 2018, https://www.nytimes.com/2018/12/05/climate/greenhouse-gas-emissions-2018.html.

32   Bob Berwyn, "Ice Loss and the Polar Vortex: How a Warming Arctic Fuels Cold Snaps," InsideClimate News, September 28, 2017, https://insideclimatenews.org/news/27092017/polar-vortex-cold-snap-arctic-ice-loss-global-warming-climate-change.

33   Carolyn Gramling, "4 Ways to Put the 100-Degree Arctic Heat Record in Context," Science News, July 1, 2020, accessed July 6, 2020, https://www.sciencenews.org/article/climate-new-high-temperature-heat-record-arctic-siberia-context.

34   Oliver Milman et al., "The Unseen Driver behind the Migrant Caravan: Climate Change," Guardian (US edition), October 30, 2018, https://www.theguardian.com/world/2018/oct/30/migrant-caravan-causes-climate-change-central-america.

35   Robert Henson, The Rough Guide to Climate Change: The Symptoms, the Science, the Solutions (London: Rough Guides, 2011), 19.

35   Bill McKibben, Falter: Has the Human Game Begun to Play Itself Out? (New York: Henry Holt, 2019), 76.

36   Bob Silberg, "Why a Half-Degree Temperature Is a Big Deal," NASA, June 29, 2016, https://climate.nasa.gov/news/2458/why-a-half-degree-temperature-rise-is-a-big-deal/.

38   Mychaylo Prystupa, "At COP21, Oil Sands Worker Urges Smooth Transition off Fossil Fuels," Mychaylo (blog), December 2018, http://mychaylo.com/portfolio/at-cop21-oil-sands-mechanic-urges-shift-away-from-fossil-fuels/.

38   Prystupa.

39   Coral Davenport, "Nations Approve Landmark Climate Accord in Paris," New York Times, December 12, 2015, https://www.nytimes.com/2015/12/13/world/europe/climate-change-accord-paris.html.

39   Davenport.

39   Michael D. Shear, "Trump Will Withdraw U.S. from Paris Climate Agreement," New York Times, June 1, 2017, https://www.nytimes.com/2017/06/01/climate/trump-paris-climate-agreement.html.

39   Shear.

39   Mary Robinson, Climate Justice: Hope, Resilience, and the Fight for a Sustainable Future (New York: Bloomsbury, 2018), 131.

39   Shear, "Trump."

40   Chelsea Harvey, "Scientists Can Now Blame Individual Natural Disasters on Climate Change," Scientific America, ClimateWire, January 2, 2018, https://www.scientificamerican.com/article/scientists-can-now-blame-individual-natural-disasters-on-climate-change/.

42   Coral Davenport and Kendra Pierre-Louis, "U.S. Climate Report Warns of Damaged Environment and Shrinking Economy," New York Times, November 23, 2018, https://www.nytimes.com/2018/11/23/climate/us-climate-report.html.

42   Oliver Milman, "Climate Report: Trump Administration Downplays Warnings of Looming Disaster," *Guardian* (US edition), November 24, 2018, https://www.theguardian.com/environment/2018/nov/24/climate-change-report-trump-administration-democrats-reaction.

42   Milman.

44   Jeff Berardelli, "'We Are at a Crossroads': House Democrats Release Plan to Address Climate Crisis," CBS News, June 30, 2020, accessed July 5, 2020, https://www.cbsnews.com/news/climate-change-crisis-democrats-plan-house/.

44   "Pelosi Tells COP25 Summit They Can Still Count on US," RTE News, December 2, 2019, https://www.nytimes.com/2010/12/22/science/earth/22carbon.html.

44   "Pelosi Tells COP25 Summit."

45   Brian Roewe, "With Little Progress at COP25 Climate Summit, Attention Turns to 2020," EarthBeat, December 19, 2019, https://www.ncronline.org/news/earthbeat/little-progress-cop-25-climate-summit-attention-turns-2020.

45   Umair Irfan, "We Are Desperate for Any Sign of Hope," Vox, December 11, 2019, https://www.vox.com/2019/12/11/21010673/cop25-greta-thunberg-climate-change-un-meeting-madrid.

45, 47   Tara John et al., "COP25 Was Meant to Tackle the Climate Crisis. It Fell Short," CNN, December 15, 2019, https://www.cnn.com/2019/12/15/world/cop25-climate-change-intl/index.html.

46   Philip Shabecoff, "Global Warming Has Begun, Expert Tells Senate," *New York Times*, June 24, 1988, https://www.nytimes.com/1988/06/24/us/global-warming-has-begun-expert-tells-senate.html.

46   Jeanna Bryner, "NASA Climate Scientist Arrested in Pipeline Protest," NBC News, February 13, 2013, http://www.nbcnews.com/id/50805486/ns/technology_and_science-science/t/nasa-climate-scientist-arrested-pipeline-protest/#.XjmmrGhKi70.

47   Andrea Germanos, "'We Are Unstoppable, Another World Is Possible!': Young Climate Activists Storm COP25 Stage," Common Dreams, December 22, 2019, https://www.commondreams.org/news/2019/12/11/we-are-unstoppable-another-world-possible-young-climate-activists-storm-cop-25-stage.

48   Rachel Nunes, "Raimondo Calls for Complete Change to Renewable Energy by 2030," Patch.com, January 17, 2020, https://patch.com/rhode-island/cranston/raimondo-calls-complete-change-renewable-energy-2030.

49   Alex Kuffner, "Examining Raimondo's Goal: Can R.I. Reach 100% Renewable Power by 2030?," *Newport (RI) Journal*, January 16, 2020, https://www.newportri.com/news/20200116/examining-raimondos-goal-can-ri-reach-100-renewable-power-by-2030.

50   "Can the World Run on Renewable Energy," Wharton, University of
       Pennsylvania, April 23, 2015, https://knowledge.wharton.upenn.edu/article
       /can-the-world-run-on-renewable-energy/.

51   Monica Amarelo, "Path to 100 Percent Renewable Energy Is Here," EWG,
       March 26, 2019, https://www.ewg.org/energy/release/22508/path-100
       -percent-renewable-energy-here.

51–52 Ken Caldeira et al., "Top Climate Change Scientists' Letter to Policy
        Influencers," CNN, last modified November 3, 2013, https://www.cnn
        .com/2013/11/03/world/nuclear-energy-climate-change-scientists-letter
        /index.html.

54   Adam Popescu, "This Scientist Thinks She Has the Key to Curb Climate
       Change: Super Plants," *Guardian* (US edition), April 16, 2019, https://www
       .theguardian.com/environment/2019/apr/16/super-plants-climate-change
       -joanne-chory-carbon-dioxide.

55   Kenyon College, "Wetlands Play Vital Role in Carbon Storage, Study
       Finds," Phys.org, February 2, 2017, https://phys.org/news/2017-02-wetlands
       -vital-role-carbon-storage.html.

57   Sarah Bliss, "Could Hawaii Be Paradise for Hydrogen-Powered Public
       Transit?" *Bloomberg CityLab*, April 22, 2019, accessed June 25, 2020, https://
       www.bloomberg.com/news/articles/2019-04-22/hawaii-s-hydrogen-powered
       -bus-could-be-a-big-deal.

58   Eric Holthaus, "Why I'm Never Flying Again," Quartz, October 1, 2013,
       https://qz.com/129477/why-im-never-flying-again/.

61   Justin Gillis, "A Scientist, His Work, and a Climate Reckoning," *New York
       Times*, December 21, 2010, https://www.nytimes.com/2010/12/22/science
       /earth/22carbon.html.

63   Eli Kintisch, "Born to Rewild: A Father and Son's Quest to Bring Back a
       Lost Ecosystem—and Save the World," *Science*, December 4, 2015, https://
       science.sciencemag.org/content/350/6265/1148.abstract.

65   Ben Leach, "'Fake Trees' Could Fight Climate Change," *Telegraph (London)*,
       August 27, 2009, https://www.telegraph.co.uk/news/science/science
       -news/609770.

66   John Schwartz, "Wallace Broecker, 87, Dies; Sounded Early Warning on
       Climate Change," *New York Times*, February 19, 2019, https://www.nytimes
       .com/2019/02/19/obituaries/wallace-broecker-dead.html.

66   James Rainey, "Wallace Smith Broecker, the 'Grandfather' of Climate
       Science, Leaves a Final Warning for Earth," NBC News, March 3, 2019,
       https://www.nbcnews.com/news/us-news/grandfather-climate-science-leaves
       -final-warning-earth-n978426.

67   Jan Wesner Childs, "Energy Companies Investing Heavily in Carbon
       Capture Technology," The Weather Channel, April 4, 2019, https://weather
       .com/news/climate/news/2019-04-04-carbon-engineering-capture-carbon
       -dioxide-emissions.

68   Trevor Nace, "Scientists Just Pulled CO_2 from Air and Turned It into Coal," *Forbes*, February 27, 2019, https://www.forbes.com/sites/trevornace/2019 /02/27/scientists-just-pulled-co2-from-air-and-turned-it-into-coal /#6146db5f4563.

69   Hugh Powell, "Fertilizing the Ocean with Iron," *Oceanus Magazine*, November 13, 2007, https://www.whoi.edu/oceanus/feature/fertilizing-the -ocean-with-iron/.

70   Brian Kahn, "Giant Space Mirrors, Engineered Glaciers: Presidential Candidate Andrew Yang Shares His Wildest Plans for Fighting Climate Change," *Earther*, March 29, 2019, https://earther.gizmodo.com/giant-space -mirrors-engineered-glaciers-presidential-1833669977.

71   "Explainer: Six Ideas to Limit Global Warming with Solar Geoengineering," Carbon Brief, May 9, 2018, https://www.carbonbrief.org/explainer-six-ideas -to-limit-global-warming-with-solar-geoengineering.

71   Jon Gernter, "The Tiny Swiss Company That Thinks It Can Help Stop Climate Change," *New York Times Magazine*, February 12, 2019, https:// www.nytimes.com/2019/02/12/magazine/climeworks-business-climate -change.html.

72   Jeff Goodell, *The Water Will Come: Rising Seas, Sinking Cities, and the Remaking of the Civilized World* (New York: Little, Brown, 2017), 185–186.

74   Oliver Milman and Mae Ryan, "Lives in the Balance: Climate Change and the Marshall Islands," *Guardian* (London), September 15, 2016, https:// www.theguardian.com/environment/2016/sep/15/marshall-islands-climate -change-springdale-arkansas.

75   Justin Worland, "Climate Change Has Already Increased Global Inequality. It Will Only Get Worse," *Time*, April 22, 2019, accessed July 5, 2020, https://time.com/5575523/climate-change-inequality/.

76   Lisa Friedman, "Tony de Brum, Voice of Pacific Islands on Climate Change, Dies at 72," *New York Times*, August 22, 2017, https://www.nytimes.com /2017/08/22/world/tony-de-brum-dead-climate-change-advocate.html.

76   Goodell, *Water Will Come*, 170.

76   Fiona Harvey, "Tony de Brum Obituary," *Guardian* (US edition), October 10, 2017, https://www.theguardian.com/environment/2017/oct/10/tony-de -brum-obituary.

77   Vann R. Newkirk II, "Climate Change Is Already Damaging American Democracy," *Atlantic*, October 24, 2018, https://www.theatlantic.com /politics/archive/2018/10/climate-change-damaging-american-democracy /573769/.

78   Steffen et al., "Trajectories."

79   Steffen et al.

79, 82 Chad Frischmann, "100 Solutions to Reverse Climate Warming," TED talk, accessed [tk], https://www.ted.com/talks/chad_frischmann_100_solutions _to_climate_change/transcript.

80 Gleb Raygorodetsky, "Indigenous Peoples Defend Earth's Biodiversity—but They're in Danger," *National Geographic*, November 16, 2018, https://www .nationalgeographic.com/environment/2018/11/can-indigenous-land -stewardship-protect-biodiversity-/.

80 Raygorodetsky.

81 Julie Mollins, "UN to Launch Global Campaign against Criminalization of Indigenous Peoples," Truthout, April 26, 2019, https://truthout.org/articles /un-to-launch-global-campaign-against-criminalization-of-indigenous -peoples/.

81 Alina Tugend, "How AI Can Help Handle Severe Weather," *New York Times*, May 12, 2019, https://www.nytimes.com/2019/05/12/climate /artificial-intelligence-climate-change.html.

82–83 "#Envision2030: 17 Goals to Transform the World for Persons with Disabilities," United Nations Department of Economic and Social Affairs, accessed June 25, 2020, https://www.un.org/development/desa/disabilities /envision2030.html.

83 Johan Rockström, "5 Transformational Policies for a Prosperous and Sustainable World," TED talk, September 2018, https://www.ted.com/talks /johan_rockstrom_5_transformational_policies_for_a_prosperous_and _sustainable_world/transcript.

85 Simon Fry, "The World's First Floating Farm Making Waves in Rotterdam," BBC, August 17, 2018, https://www.bbc.com/news/business-45130010.

85 Chris Bentley, "As Sea Levels Rise, Rotterdam Floats to the Top as an Example of How to Live with the Water," PRI, June 20, 2016, https://www .pri.org/stories/2016-06-20/sea-levels-rise-rotterdam-floats-top-example -how-live-water.

86 Spencer Reiss, "Climate Change Is Inevitable. Get Used to It," *Wired*, May 19, 2008, https://www.wired.com/2008/05/ff-heresies-10worst/.

86 Molly Wood, "Climate Adaptation Isn't Surrender. It's Survival," *Wired*, May 17, 2019, https://www.wired.com/story/climate-adaptation-isnt -surrender-its-survival/.

87 "World Bank Group Announces $5 Billion over Five Years for Climate Adaptation and Resilience," World Bank, January 15, 2019, https://www .worldbank.org/en/news/press-release/2019/01/15/world-bank-group -announces-50-billion-over-five-years-for-climate-adaptation-and-resilience.

88 Emily Anthes, "A Floating House to Resist the Floods of Climate Change," *New Yorker*, January 3, 2018, https://www.newyorker.com/tech/annals-of -technology/a-floating-house-to-resist-the-floods-of-climate-change.

89 Anthes.

90 Jeffrey Ball, "With Climate Change No Longer in the Future, Adaptation Speeds Up," *New York Times*, September 21, 2018, https://www.nytimes .com/2018/09/21/climate/climate-change-adaptation.html.

91   Alina Tugend, "How AI Can Help Handle Severe Weather," *New York Times*, May 12, 2019, https://www.nytimes.com/2019/05/12/climate /artificial-intelligence-climate-change.html.

92   Ron Brackett, "Marshall Islands Will Fight Sea Level Rise by Raising Islands," weather.com, February 26, 2019, https://weather.com/news /news/2019-02-26-marshall-islands-fight-sea-level-rise-raising-islands.

92   Giff Johnson, "Marshall Islands Plans to Raise Islands to Escape Sea Level Rise," RNZ, February 25, 2019, https://www.rnz.co.nz/international/pacific -news/383299/marshall-islands-plans-to-raise-islands-to-escape-sea-level-rise.

93   Hiroko Tabuchi, "Tokyo Is Preparing for Floods 'beyond Anything We've Seen,'" *New York Times*, October 6, 2017, https://www.nytimes.com/2017 /10/06/climate/tokyo-floods.html.

93   Tabuchi.

94   Li Jung, "Inside China's Leading 'Sponge City': Wuhan's War with Water," *Guardian* (US edition), January 23, 2019, https://www.theguardian.com /cities/2019/jan/23/inside-chinas-leading-sponge-city-wuhans-war-with -water.

96   Hilary Brueck, "Bill Gates and Ban Ki-moon Are Recruiting Mayors, Heads of State, and Finance Pros around the World on a Last Ditch Quest to Save Us from Catastrophic Heat, Drought, and Flooding," Business Insider, October 16, 2018, https://www.businessinsider.in/bill-gates-and-ban-ki -moon-are-recruiting-mayors-heads-of-state-and-finance-pros-around-the -world-on-a-last-minute-quest-to-save-us-from-catastrophic-heat-drought -and-flooding/articleshow/66241529.cms.

97   Damian Carrington, "Leaders Move Past Trump to Protect World from Climate Change," *Guardian* (US edition), October 16, 2016, https://www .theguardian.com/environment/2018/oct/16/leaders-move-past-trump-to -protect-world-from-climate-change.

97   Johan Rockström and Mattias Klum, *Big World, Small Planet: Abundance within Planetary Boundaries* (New Haven, CT: Yale University Press, 2015), 152.

98   Madison Dibble, "'Act as If You Loved Your Children': Greta Thunberg Trashes Leaders at World Economic Forum," *Washington Examiner*, January 21, 2020, https://www.washingtonexaminer.com/news/act-as-if-you-loved -your-children-greta-thunberg-trashes-global-leaders-at-world-economic -forum.

99   John Sexton, "Greta Thunberg: 'Immediately Halt All Investments in Fossil Fuel Exploration and Extraction," Hot Air, January 22, 2020, https://hotair .com/archives/john-s-2/2020/01/22/greta-thunberg-immediately-halt -investments-fossil-fuel-exploration-extraction/.

99   Sexton.

100   Jonathan Watts, "Greta Thunberg, Schoolgirl Climate Change Warrior: 'Some People Can Let Things Go. I Can't.'" *Guardian* (US edition), March 11, 2019, https://www.theguardian.com/world/2019/mar/11/greta-thunberg -schoolgirl-climate-change-warrior-some-people-can-let-things-go-i-cant.

100   Watts.

102   Ari Kelo, "Meet Activist Autumn Peltier: The Young 'Water Warrior' Making a Splash, Rising, October 4, 2019, http://therising.co/2019/10/04 /meet-activist-autumn-peltier-the-young-water-warrior-making-a-splash/.

102   Rachel Janfaza, "9 Climate Activists of Color You Should Know," *Teen Vogue*, January 3, 2020, https://www.teenvogue.com/story/youth-climate -activists-of-color.

102   Rebecca Nagle, "The Indigenous Teen Who Confronted Trudeau about Unsafe Water Took on the UN," *Vice*, October 1, 2019, https://www.vice .com/en_us/article/8xwvx3/the-indigenous-teen-who-confronted-trudeau -about-unsafe-water-took-on-the-un.

103   "Transcript: Greta Thunberg's Speech at the UN Climate Action Summit," NPR, September 23, 2019, https://www.npr.org/2019/09/23/763452863 /transcript-greta-thunbergs-speech-at-the-u-n-climate-action-summit.

103   Barry Hatton and Frank Jordans, AP, "Greta Thunberg Says Voyage 'Energized' Her Climate Fight," ABC News, December 3, 2019, https:// abcnews.go.com/Technology/wireStory/current-decade-heading-temperature -record-67455910.

104   Alli Maloney, "21 under 21: Jamie Margolin Knows Climate Justice Is the Key to All Justice," *Teen Vogue*, November 5, 2018, https://www.teenvogue .com/story/jamie-margolin-21-under-21-2018.

104   Kristen Doerer, "Youth Climate Activists Marched on Washington, D.C.," *Teen Vogue*, July 22, 2018, https://www.teenvogue.com/story/youth-climate -change-activists-marched-washington-dc.

104   Andrea Gonzalez-Ramirez, "Why Miami Was the Perfect Place for These Teens to Organize a Climate-Change Summit," Yahoo Lifestyle, July 11, 2019, https://www.yahoo.com/lifestyle/why-miami-perfect-place-teens -194500207.html.

105   "Greta Thunberg UN Speech at COP25 in Full," *Daily Express (London)*, December 13, 2019, https://www.express.co.uk/news/science/1216452/Greta -Thunberg-UN-speech-full-COP25-Greta-Thunberg-speech-transcript -climate-change.

105   Steve Kroft, interviewer, "The Climate Change Lawsuit That Could Stop the U.S. Government from Supporting Fossil Fuels," CBS, *60 Minutes*, June 23, 2019, https://www.cbsnews.com/news/juliana-versus-united-states -climate-change-lawsuit-60-minutes-2019-06-23/.

106   Kroft.

106   America's Founding Documents: "The Constitution of the United States," A transcription, *National Archives*, accessed, June 25, 2020, https://www.archives.gov/founding-docs/constitution-transcript.

106   America's Founding Documents.

107   Olivia Rosane, "'Where Is the Hope?' after Juliana v. U.S. Lawsuit Gets Tossed by Federal Court," EcoWatch, January 20, 2020, https://www.ecowatch.com/juliana-v-united-states-tossed-2644863188.html?rebelltitem=3#rebelltitem3.

107   Rosane.

110   Amy Eskind, "Al Gore Calls Climate a 'Life or Death Battle'—But Feels 'Good" about New Youth Leaders," *People*, November 22, 2019, https://people.com/human-interest/al-gore-climate-change-life-or-death-battle-feels-good-new-youth-leaders/?utm=newsbreak.

111   Emily Witt, "The Optimistic Activists for a Green New Deal: Inside the Youth-Led Singing Sunrise Movement," *New Yorker*, December 23, 2018, https://www.newyorker.com/news/news-desk/the-optimistic-activists-for-a-green-new-deal-inside-the-youth-led-singing-sunrise-movement.

111   Osita Nwanevu, "A Decisive Year for the Sunrise Movement and the Green New Deal," *New Yorker*, May 14, 2019, https://www.newyorker.com/news/our-columnists/a-decisive-year-for-the-sunrise-movement-and-the-green-new-deal.

112   Emma Brockes, "When Alexandria Ocasio-Cortez Met Greta Thunberg: 'Hope Is Contagious,'" *Guardian* (US edition), June 29, 2019, https://www.theguardian.com/environment/2019/jun/29/alexandria-ocasio-cortez-met-greta-thunberg-hope-contagious-climate.

113   Tedros Adhanom Ghebreyesus, "WHO Director-General's Opening Remarks at the Media Briefing on COVID-19—21 August 2020," World Health Organization, August 21, 2020, https://www.who.int/dg/speeches/detail/who-director-general-s-opening-remarks-at-the-media-briefing-on-covid-19---21-august-2020.

SELECTED BIBLIOGRAPHY

Berners-Lee, Mike. *There Is No Planet B: A Handbook for the Make or Break Years.* Cambridge: Cambridge University Press, 2019.

Goodell, Jeff. *The Water Will Come: Rising Seas, Sinking Cities, and the Remaking of the Civilized World.* New York: Little, Brown, 2017.

Gore, Al. *An Inconvenient Truth: The Planetary Emergency of Global Warming and What We Can Do about It.* New York: Rodale, 2006.

———. *Truth to Power: An Inconvenient Sequel.* New York: Rodale, 2017.

Hawken, Paul, ed. *Drawdown: The Most Comprehensive Plan Ever Proposed to Reverse Global Warming.* New York: Penguin Books, 2017.

Henson, Robert. *The Rough Guide to Climate Change: The Symptoms, the Science, the Solutions.* London: Rough Guides, 2011.

———. *The Thinking Person's Guide to Climate Change.* Boston: American Meteorological Society, 2014.

Jamal, Dahr. *The End of Ice: Bearing Witness and Finding Meaning in the Path of Climate Disruption.* New York: New Press, 2019.

Kolbert, Elizabeth. *Field Notes from a Catastrophe: Man, Nature, and Climate Change.* New York: Bloomsbury, 2006.

McKibben, Bill. *Eaarth: Making a Life on a Tough New Planet.* New York: St. Martin's Griffin, 2010.

———. *Falter: Has the Human Game Begun to Play Itself Out?* New York: Henry Holt, 2019.

Rich, Nathaniel. *Losing Earth: A Recent History.* New York: Farrar, Straus and Giroux, 2019.

Robinson, Mary. *Climate Justice: Hope, Resilience, and the Fight for a Sustainable Future.* New York: Bloomsbury, 2018.

Rockström, Johan, and Mattias Klum. *Big World, Small Planet: Abundance within Planetary Boundaries.* New Haven, CT: Yale University Press, 2015.

Smith, Lawrence C. *The World in 2050: Four Forces Shaping Civilization's Northern Future.* New York: Penguin Group, 2011.

Steffen, Will, Johan Rockström, Katherine Richardson, Timothy M. Lenton, Carl Folke, Diana Liverman, Colin P. Summerhayes et al. "Trajectories of the Earth System in the Anthropocene," *Proceedings of the National Academy of Sciences of the United States of America* 115, no. 33 (August 14, 2018): 8252–8259.

Ticknell, Josh. *Kiss the Ground: How the Food You Eat Can Reverse Climate Change, Heal Your Body & Ultimately Save Our World*. New York: Enliven Books, 2017.

Wallace-Wells, David. *The Uninhabitable Earth: Life after Warming*. New York: Tim Duggan Books, 2019.

Walsh, Brian. *Global Warming: The Causes, The Perils, The Solutions*. New York: Time Books, 2012.

FURTHER INFORMATION

BOOKS

Collins, Anna. *The Climate Change Crisis*. Farmington Hills, MI: Lucent, 2018.
Read information on climate change, the causes of climate denial, and action for minimizing the worst effects of climate change.

Flannery, Tim. Adapted by Sally M. Walker "for the Generation Who Will Act on Global Warming." *We Are the Weather Makers: The History of Climate Change*. Somerville, MA: Candlewick, 2010.
This young reader's edition of Flannery's 2006 adult title, *The Weather Makers*, covers the history of climate change and offers twenty-five tips for helping the environment.

Fleischman, Paul. *Eyes Wide Open: Going beyond the Environmental Headlines*. Somerville, MA: Candlewick, 2014.
This book provides an insightful look at the science, politics, history, and psychology of climate change.

Foxxe, Ellen. *The Rising Seas: Shorelines under Threat*. New York: Rosen, 2006.
Read about the hardships and coping strategies of people whose homes are endangered by rising sea levels.

Gillard, Arthur. *Climate Change*. Farmington Hills, MI: Greenhaven, 2011.
An overall picture of climate change and what needs to be done to stop it.

Hand, Carol. *Climate Change: Our Warming Earth*. Edina, MN: Abdo, 2015.
Learn more about the causes of climate change, climate denial, and measures to lessen the effects of climate change.

Hirsch, Rebecca E. *Climate Migrants: On the Move in a Warming World*. Minneapolis: Twenty-First Century Books, 2016.
Hirsch's thought-provoking book deals with the plight of people forced to leave their homes by rising sea levels, droughts, catastrophic weather events, or other results of climate change.

Johnson, Jordan. *From Kyoto to Paris*. New York: Cavendish Square, 2018.
Johnson discusses the history of international climate pacts and explains how governments are trying to safeguard the environment.

Lloyd, Saci. *The Carbon Diaries 2015*. New York: Holiday House, 2009.
In this novel, accelerating climate change causes the United Kingdom to institute carbon rationing as sixteen-year-old Laura deals with personal and environmental turmoil.

Sivertsen, Linda, and Tosh Sivertsen. *Generation Green: The Ultimate Teen Guide to Living an Eco-Friendly Life.* New York: Simon Pulse, 2008.
Written by a mother with her teenage son, *Generation Green* includes scientific material, interviews with teens and celebrities, and advice for living a green lifestyle.

Slaven, Marissa. *Code Blue.* Coquitlam, BC: Moon Willow, 2018.
Labeled an "eco-mystery," this novel is set in a future where climate change has greatly altered the world.

Streissguth, Thomas. *Extreme Weather.* Farmington Hills, MI: Greenhaven, 2010.
Learn about the ways that climate change and severe weather affect health, the spread of infectious diseases, and food supplies.

Swanson, Jennifer. *Geoengineering Earth's Climate: Resetting the Thermostat.* Minneapolis: Twenty-First Century Books, 2017.
Swanson provides thorough coverage of the different forms of geoengineering, carefully weighing the pros and cons.

Tillman, Ted. *The Big Melt.* Columbia, MD: South Branch, 2018.
In this futuristic novel, Marley and Brianna must deal with climate disasters that strike the day after their high school graduation.

FILMS

Before the Flood. Written by Mark Monroe. Directed by Fisher Stevens. Washington, DC: National Geographic Films, 2016.
Watch UN messenger of peace Leonardo DiCaprio travel around the world investigating environmental problems.

Chasing Coral. Written by Davis Coombe, Vicki Curtis, and Jeff Orlowski. Directed by Jeff Orlowski. Boulder, CO: Exposure Labs, 2017.
Learn about the work of scientists, divers, and photographers who study the impact of climate change and ocean acidification on coral reefs.

Chasing Ice. Written by Mark Monroe. Directed by Jeff Orlowski. Boulder, CO: Exposure Labs, 2013.
Follow National Geographic photographer and former climate change skeptic James Balog as he documents the accelerated melting of glaciers in Greenland, Iceland, and Alaska.

Climate Change: The Facts. Presented by Sir David Attenborough. Directed by Serena Davies. London: BBC Studios and IWC Media, 2019.
Broadcaster and natural historian David Attenborough discusses the causes of and possible solutions to climate change.

The Day after Tomorrow. Written by Roland Emmerich and Jeffrey Nachmanoff. Directed by Roland Emmerich. Beverly Hills, CA: Twentieth Century Fox Home Entertainment, 2009.
As climate change worsens, a scientist tries to solve the problem in this fictional movie.

Ice on Fire. Narrated by Leonardo DiCaprio. Directed by Leila Conners. West Hollywood, CA: Appian Way Productions, 2019.
Discover ways to slow down climate change. The film offers hope that the worst effects may yet be avoided.

An Inconvenient Sequel: Truth to Power. Written by Al Gore. Directed by Jon Shenk and Bonni Cohen. Hollywood, CA: Paramount Pictures, 2017.
This film updates Gore's previous pioneering film, *An Inconvenient Truth*, with evidence that climate change is increasing.

An Inconvenient Truth. Written by Al Gore. Directed by Davis Guggenheim. Hollywood, CA: Paramount, 2006.
Al Gore's groundbreaking documentary presents compelling scientific evidence for climate change and discusses the political issues surrounding it.

The Island President. Written by Jon Shenk. Directed by Jon Shenk. New York: First Run Features, 2012.
Follow President Mohamed Nasheed of the Maldives as he fights to save his nation from climate change.

This Changes Everything. Written by Naomi Klein. Directed by Avi Lewis. New York: Message Productions, 2015.
Visit seven communities on the forefront of climate change, and learn what they are doing to survive.

Tomorrow. Written and directed by Cyril Dion and Melanie Laurent. Warren, NJ: Passion River, 2017.
Find out what communities around the globe are doing to solve environmental problems and combat climate change.

WEBSITES

Climate Central
https://www.climatecentral.org/
Read multiple accounts discussing the impact of climate change.

The Climate Change Guide
https://www.climate-change-guide.com/
Learn about the impacts of climate change and what can be done to lessen its effects.

The Intergovernmental Panel on Climate Change
https://www.ipcc.ch/
Discover a wealth of information on the reports and the workings of the IPCC.

Kids against Climate Change
https://kidsagainstclimatechange.co/start-learning/
Find general information, actions one can take to help the environment, games, and activities.

Kids Can Save the Planet
http://kidscansavetheplanet.com/
The site includes information and trailers for films in teenage filmmaker Dylan D'Haeze's environmental documentary series *Kids Can Save the Planet*.

NASA Climate Kids
https://climatekids.nasa.gov/menu/dream/
Read about a variety of topics including weather and climate, atmosphere, energy, and plants and animals. The site also includes activities, videos, and games.

National Geographic Kids: Climate Change
https://kids.nationalgeographic.com/explore/science/climate-change/
Besides good general information, this site includes a glossary, a list of ways to help the environment, and links to articles on saving Earth.

Sustainable Development Goals: Goal 13—Take Urgent Action to Combat Climate Change and Its Impacts
https://www.un.org/sustainabledevelopment/climate-change/
Read about the UN climate summits, the Paris Agreement, the IPCC Climate Report of 2018, and frequently asked questions.

Youth for Climate Action
https://unfccc.int/topics/education-and-outreach/workstreams/youth
-engagement
Explore what young people across the globe are doing to fight climate change, and read lists of youth activities and events at UN Climate Change Conferences.

INDEX

ABOUT THE AUTHOR

Stephanie Sammartino Mcpherson wrote her first children's story in college. She enjoyed the process so much that she's never stopped writing. A former teacher and freelance newspaper writer, she has written more than thirty books and numerous magazine stories. Her recent books include *The Global Refugee Crisis: Fleeing Conflict and Violence* and *Arctic Thaw: Climate Change and the Global Race for Energy Resources.* She and her husband, Richard, live in Virginia but also call California home.

PHOTO ACKNOWLEDGMENTS

Image credits: VINCENT MAYANJA/AFP/Getty Images, p. 5; PETER BUSOMOKE/AFP/Getty Images, p. 6; ATTILA KISBENEDEK/AFP/Getty Images, p. 7; Laura Westlund/Independent Picture Service, pp. 8, 10, 13, 21, 32, 89, 95; PGEGiEK/Wikimedia Commons (CC BY-SA 4.0), p. 9; William Anders/ NASA/JSC, p. 16; NASA/OIB/Jeremy Harbeck, p. 19; Andre Vieira/MCT/Tribune News Service/Getty Images, p. 23; Stephen Frink/Getty Images, p. 25; joe daniel price/Moment/Getty Images, p. 31; Ayhan Mehmet/Anadolu Agency/Getty Images, p. 33; Nicolas Economou/NurPhoto/Getty Images, p. 37; Chip Somodevilla/ Getty Images, p. 43; U.S. Army Photo, p. 50; KIMIMASA MAYAMA/AFP/Getty Images, p. 52; MICHELE SIBILONI/AFP/Getty Images, p. 55; Rhonda Roth/ Shutterstock.com, p. 57; AP Photo/Arthur Max, p. 64; Arizona State University, p. 65; NASA, p. 70; GIFF JOHNSON/AFP/Getty Images, p. 73; National Archives, p. 74; AVENTURIER/Gamma-Rapho/Getty Images, p. 75; NASA/CIESIN, p. 77; UNDR/Shutterstock.com, p. 81; Nacho Calonge/Getty Images, p. 85; Ziaul Haque Oisharjh/SOPA Images/LightRocket/Getty Images, p. 87; Paul Rawlingson/ Shutterstock.com, p. 88; Kumiko Hirama/Shutterstock.com, p. 93; Wang Jianhua/ Xinhua/Alamy Live News, p. 94; Ronald Patrick/Getty Images, p. 99; REUTERS/ Arnd Wiegmann/Newscom, p. 102; Barbara Alper/Getty Images, p. 103; Alex Wong/ Getty Images, p. 106; Alexandros Michailidis/Shutterstock.com, p. 109.

Cover image: istock/Getty Images.